Online Teaching

Learn to Set up the Zoom App, its Features, and Strategies for Effectively Conducting Online Classes

By

Martha Avrith

The trademarks that are used are without any consent, and the publication of the trademark is without permission or backing by the trademark owner. All trademarks and brands within this book are for clarifying purposes only and are owned by the owners themselves, not affiliated with this document.

Table of contents

Introduction

Zoom Video Conference Application is an American technology services corporation based in California. It offers video telecommunications and online messaging facilities via one-on-one computing network located in the cloud, used for video conferencing, teleworking, online education, and social interaction. Zoom's model focuses on a product that is easier to use than the previous ones. Moreover, it is better regarding pricing advantages, which include reduced infrastructure-level hardware costs, ensuring a workforce productivity.

With the adoption of prevention steps introduced in reaction to this scenario globally, Zoom's device use has seen a substantial global rise beginning in early 2020. The software applications have been subject to criticism by the public and media due to privacy and security concerns. A portion of the Zoom staff is centered in China, which has contributed significantly to monitoring and surveillance concerns.

With the rise in the Zoom video conference in this global scenario, people are using Zoom for their personal and private use. Remote working and distance education are much more comfortable with the Zoom application. You need to download and install the application on your desktop, Mac devices, or smartphone. Creating an account and sign in to Zoom from your device is more straightforward, and you can use multiple methods to get started with your Zoom application discussed in detail in this book.

Zoom is easy to use, and its pricing is affordable if you are a teacher and want to give classes online. It has four plans with an additional plan of education that is mainly for instructors. Now more teachers use tools like Zoom to meet their learners. While many teachers use this opportunity to teach or discuss the curriculum for their learners, many use Zoom meetings just for social interaction.

Now that distance education has become the latest standard for teachers worldwide; innovation is at an all-time peak as educators continue to find out how to meet their learners' educational needs and how to educate them. For that, zooming may be a fantastic choice. If you have never experienced Zoom before, trying it out on the way can be confusing, so we have put up all in this book that you need to learn along with to get you moving.

This book will help you to learn the basics of the Zoom application with its first introductory chapter. It will further guide you about Zoom features and how you can use these features for your video conferencing. In the second chapter, a detailed procedure has been given about downloading, installing, and creating an account for Zoom. It will assist you in hosting your meetings, webinars, and classes with different Zoom tools. The third chapter is all about teaching with Zoom and best practices. It also includes Assignment and presentation setups to enhance your teaching skills through Zoom. Chapter four will discuss the benefits of Zoom application software and its comparison with other meeting applications to clear your understanding if you have any confusion for selecting Zoom over others. The last chapter is all about tips and tricks to make your Zoom video conference more effective. Thus, start reading this book to learn more about Zoom.

Chapter 1: Understanding Zoom and its Features

Technology for video conferencing is the backbone of every efficient and effective team. Video conference tools, such as Zoom; it allows individuals to connect and meet together in a "face-to-face" manner effectively when interacting in person is not possible. That makes interacting much more individual centrally, which is essential to help users feel linked and stay in touch.

Zoom is a cloud-based video conference application that can be used for audio conferencing, video conferences, webinars, broadcasting conferences, and live chat. According to the study, after Skype for Industry, Zoom is perhaps the most successful video conferencing tool for businesses with five hundred or fewer employees and the second-most common solution for companies, including over five hundred employees. In 2019 over half of Fortune five-hundred companies officially used Zoom and reached even higher heights during 2020, citing three-hundred million daily Zoom attendees recently.

Typically, when people talk about Zoom, Zoom Session, and Zoom Room. A Zoom Meeting refers to a meeting that holds a video conference using Zoom. You can attend such meetings via a webcam or mobile. In the meantime, a Zoom Room is the hardware system that enables businesses from their conference rooms to schedule and initiate Zoom Meetings.

1.1 Video Conferencing with Zoom

One of the leading companies in the web conferencing orbit, Zoom, is known worldwide for its outstanding conference room's alternatives.

You would not be disappointed with Zoom when you're demanding top quality video, extraordinary functionality, and dependability. In recent times, before their Public Offering was introduced in August 2019, Zoom confirmed a whole host of new features for their selling, including notifications to Zoom conferences, updated Zoom Rooms, and, of course, the developed Zoom Phone expertise.

A "Zoom Meeting" refers simply to a conference that is held using Zoom, and participants can enter the meeting in person, either by webcam or video chat camera or by phone. A Zoom Room is the actual hardware system that enables businesses to initiate Zoom Meetings from their lecture halls. Zoom Rooms is a software-defined tool and video conferencing device for a lecture room that allows users to plan, start, and run Zoom Meetings by pressing a button. Zoom Rooms require extra membership in addition to a Zoom membership, and it is a perfect option for more influential organizations with more staff attending daily Zoom meetings.

1.2 Zoom Pricing Plans

Zoom can vary slightly based on whether you are on a desktop or a mobile device. Four packages are accessible; the most common now probably to be the free tier, where virtual meetings with up to a hundred participants can be held; face - to - face meetings are feasible without a specified time. Meetings with different members can be held for up to forty minutes (when your time is up, you can revive your session if you need to). The free choice also allows users to hold High definition meetings, and with audio, members can participate through their Computer or a phone line, and they can share screens and applications.

Zoom's Consumer, Business, and Enterprise plan come with additional functionality, including duration limits, cloud capturing and processing, connectivity of TeamViewer, single sign-in choices, and businesses' marketing. It is possible to enter a conference just from your phone, but you should install the software for stability and avoid device restrictions.

Zoom facilitates one-to-one chat sessions that can evolve into group calls, international and domestic audience coaching sessions and webinars, and international video meetings of up to one thousand participants and as many as forty-nine videos on-screen. The free tier provides unlimited one-on-one meetings but restricts community sessions to forty minutes and a hundred people. Paid pricing starts at fifteen dollars a month per host. Zoom has four price ranges to offer:

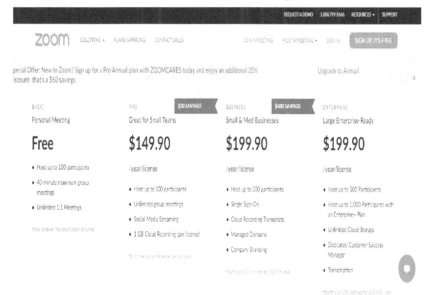

Zoom Free

Zoom is free to this stage. There is an infinite number of meetings you can attend. Group meetings are limited at forty minutes, with several members, and meetings cannot be registered.

Zoom Pro

This tier costs fifteen dollars or twelve pounds a month, as well as a host meeting. It enables hosts to create personal meeting IDs for repeated Zoom Meetings and facilitates cloud or computer recording meetings, but it limits community meeting times at twenty-four hours.

Business Zoom

This level costs twenty dollars or sixteen pounds a month and host meetings (minimum ten). It allows you to mark Zoom meetings with URLs and company logos, and it provides transcripts of cloud-recorded Zoom meetings and outstanding customer service.

Zoom Enterprise

This tier costs twenty dollars or sixteen pounds per month per meeting host (minimum hundred) and is designed for companies with a thousand plus workforce. It provides free cloud recording capacity, a customer service manager, and a webinar with zoom room promotions.

Zoom Phone Pricing

The Zoom Phone can be purchased as an insert-on to your current Zoom provider. Pricing starts from ten pounds a month, per customer for a mobile feature with voice, video, texting, emails, conferences, video conferences, etc. You can receive multiple calls over cellular data or links to wireless. In addition, Zoom is accessible via native Mac OS, Windows, iOS, and Android applications. Since all standard Zoom orders come to access financial toll-free numbers, a sound strategy is also accessible for price levels starting at hundred pounds per month. The proper plan allows users to upload request out numbers, regional dial-in figures, and international toll-free numbers for different countries. Attendees on any device are free of cost, so you can and choose regions of the world that suit you.

1.3 Zoom Education Plan

In school, video communications offer access to increased teaching tools, learner versatility, Global exchange of income, and equal opportunities to teachers and students, no matter where they are. College and staff powers are offered with different services, including educational services plan, preparation, and promotions. With the introduction of the network, education is increasingly interactive with students.

Zoom immediately eliminates the forty-minute time limit on free Basic accounts for impacted middle and high schools during this situation. With stable video collaboration systems for hybrid classes, working hours, administrative meetings, and more, Zoom helps colleges and schools boost student outcomes. With flexible Education plans starting at twenty hosts for eighteen-hundred dollars a year, they provide a solution to suit the school's needs.

Interaction and Students' Learning

Digital tutoring, counseling, career counseling, work conditions, training sessions, and mentoring provide students with ways to learn in the online classroom via Zoom.

Hybrid and Digital Classrooms

Zoom develops and extends classes using efficient networking tools, including virtual breakout rooms, multi-sharing, voting, and community chats. It creates and reconstitutes video material into host videos easily understood and allows students to learn at their speed.

Communications with the University and School Systems

Cost-efficient connectivity to cloud meeting rooms allows administrative personnel and teachers throughout the school and district to collaborate face-to-face to increase collaboration and communication.

Hardware for Enhancing the Teaching Experience

Educators should implement technology solutions that can significantly boost everybody's teaching and learning experience. Zoom suggests a range of accessories to help students and teachers feel more integrated, from classroom environments to technologies that facilitate interactive or mixed learning.

1.4 Setup Requirements for Zoom

There are some Zoom app requirements to be download or be supported on some specific hardware and operating systems. These requirements are;

System Requirements

- An Internet access-wired or wireless broadband (3G or 4G/LTE).

- Speakers and a microphone-Bluetooth wired or USB socket-in or broadband.

- A webcam or High definition screen-built-in socket-in or USB.

- Video Recording Card High definition camcorder or High definition video camera.

Bandwidth Requirements

- 2.0 megabits per second for a single screen, up and down

- 2.0 megabits per second up 4.0 megabits per second for dual-screen

- 2.0 megabits per second down 6.0 megabits per second for triple-screen

- Only for screen sharing: 150 to 300 kilo-bits per second

- For VoIP audio: 60-80 kilo-bits per second

Zoom-Rooms Platform Requirements

- The Minimum Operating system is Mac OS X 10.10 or better for mac OS.

- Windows 7, up to higher

- Hardware specifications for the Mac OS or Windows OS are Intel Core i5 or higher laptop CPU (singular screen) CPU 2.5 GHz, a double-core.

- 2.8 GHz Intel Core i7 quad-core Processor (and dual multiple screen) or higher laptop CPU (The double-bank RAM to do better).

Supported Operating Systems

- Mac Operating System X with Mac Operating System 10.9 or later

- Ubuntu 12.04 or higher

- Mint 17.1 or higher

- Windows 8 or 8.1

- Windows 7

- Cent Operating System 6.4 or higher

- Windows 10*

- Fedora 21 or higher

- Oracle Linux 6.4 or higher

- Red Hat Linux 6.4 or higher

- Arch Linux (64-bit only)

1.5 Features of Zoom App

Countless technical staff now operate from home during the current scenario, but it does not suggest business can't continue as it used to do before, just because of the technology such as video conferencing. These considering options and reviewing functionality are bombarded with choices like Connect, Google voice, and Zoom to determine which video conferencing software is for their desires. These features are strong reasons to check it out for those contemplating or even looking at Zoom. Zoom's price point is fantastic, too, as you can hold meetings of up to a hundred people without spending a penny.

Zoom Virtual Backgrounds

Zoom has the potential to fill the room around you with a picture of your selection, which requires no special camera. It works with owners of the Zoom laptop and iOS, but android phones are out of luck. The hardware components are a bit too high, but simulated backgrounds can still be used by those who do not approach them, although performance can differ. This is an excellent innovation for those working away from home who may not have the meeting rooms or who prefer to feel a little messy in their workplace. Turning it on or off is quick and having a personal context is as easy as doing a few taps.

To allow all users in the profile to have Virtual Background:

1. Log in as an operator to the Zoom website with the authorization to change account configurations.

2. Click "Account Management" and then account details in the navigation menu.

3. Move to the "Virtual Context" alternative in the "Meeting" window, and check that the configuration is disabled.

4. If the configuration is deactivated, press the activate switch.

5. If a notification dialog is shown, click "Switch On" to check the update.

6. Select "Manage Virtual Backdrop" to import user-available background photos by default.

Appearance Touch-Up

This functionality is so well implemented that in Zoom screen or iOS, you might not even know it is switched on. Located in the camera, the control panel is an area where you can adjust "Touch up My Appearance". It essentially places a hard-to-notice layer on the monitor to smooth out wrinkles, erase blemishes, and make you look a little more flawless than you would normally do. This feature is great for those early mornings when you need to attend a mandatory meeting, but you may still have some sleep or mess on your face.

Zoom Web Client

Zoom has a mobile interface for those who do not like to mess with the Zoom application or those who only want to access the conferences with other users. It is easy to use and operate with the consumer who has an insufficient desire to change configurations, making it ideal for most remote staff. It is not a default choice to allow Zoom group members to participate from their browser, so conference managers or Zoom managers (in the case of paying company accounts) would need to activate this feature in the Zoom web interface.

To access your profile, go to "Your Account" at the top-right of the Zoom page. Information such as your initials, photo, predefined conference ID, password, and local time can be updated under the "Profile" tab. First, go to "Settings."

Here you can change the default configuration, including whether or not recording is automatically activated when you or attendees attend a meeting; whether participants are allowed to join a planned meeting before the host appears or to wait for the appearance of the host.

You must ensure that you use good passwords throughout the purposes of protection and deter fraud artists from hijacking a conference. Passwords are not always installed by default, but an outbreak of security changes was made, including allowing passwords for planned, immediate, and personal meetings by extension.

Zoom Marketplace

A friendly, modern forum for teamwork will incorporate other tools and apps, and Zoom is no unique. The Zoom Platform has many modules for items like Gmail, Messenger, SharePoint, and other popular business applications that can make it more of a tool for video conferences. At-home employees who spend more time in Zoom are indeed expected to take a peek at the Zoom market. It will make it easier to plan, invite, and log certain facets of Zoom conferences.

Meeting Transcription

Zoom meeting capturing capabilities are great as all that an operator needs to do is to press a few keys to grab a screenshot from a video conference, and you'll have a database of all that occurs.

Meeting recording is also more convenient for customers with a paying Zoom Business, Educational, or Corporate account; Zoom will automatically transpose the recorded meeting records to the cloud.

A Zoom manager would turn on automated meeting translation, so make sure that it is set up correctly before beginning a meeting that you wish to translate and log.

For remote staff who have logistical problems, decide to skip a briefing, or want to be ready to look back to what is being said before having to click through a clip to find the correct time, this can significantly benefit. Unfortunately, it is not available for a basic-version for Zoom clients.

Screen Sharing

You can display the following material while being in a conference:

- Full-screen computer or phone
- A split-phase
- A part of your display
- Whiteboard
- Sound Device
- Second-camera material
- Display of iPhone/iPad

The host may deactivate the capacity to exchange their screen with attendees. Display sharing is established only for the host by extension for unlimited/basic accounts. Just the host, founder-hosts, and panel members may share their display in a webinar. When you're the computer user, the Zoom screens may be displayed throughout screen sharing. The host of the meeting can allow the participants to share their screen or not. Without the permission of the host no participant can share his screen. To share screen:

1. Select the button next to "Share Screen" inside the "Zoom Session".

2. Click "Enhanced Sharing Settings".

3. Click on Share with "Each Participant".

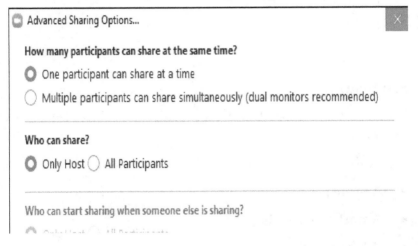

When people start sharing their screen, the conference's control systems will begin moving into a tab that can be dragged around your display.

- Start/Stop clip: start and stop the clip in-meeting.

- Mute/unmute: your headset would be silent or unmute.

- Share Pause: stop your accessed screen for the moment.

- Annotate/Whiteboard: Display sketching tools, change text, etc.

- Attendees/Manage attendees: view the attendees or monitor them.

- New Share: begin a new shared screen. You will be urged to choose which display you wish to share.

Non-Verbal Input Function

Suppose the meeting coordinator activates the Nonverbal input function. In that case, meeting attendees can place an icon next to their names to connect with the host and other attendees without interrupting the meeting stream. Tapping "Raise Hands", for example, positions the hand icon next to your name to trigger a hand raise. Both members can use the icons selected by someone else. Additionally, the host sees a rundown of how many respondents per icon shows and has the choice of eliminating all input.

To provide nonverbal reviews for all the organization's members:

1. Sign in as an admin to the Zoom online server with the ability to change account settings.

2. Click "User Settings".

3. Go to "Password Security".

4. Navigate to the "Meeting" section.

5. In-Meeting, test to allow "Nonverbal Feedback".

6. When the feature is deactivated, press the activate switch.

7. Press "Switch On" to validate the update, when a check dialog is shown.

8. If you would like to make this configuration compulsory for all users in your profile, select "Lock" to check the configuration.

To allow for your use of the Nonverbal responses feature:

1. Log in to the website for Zoom.

2. Select "Account Management" and go to "Account Configuration".

3. Move to the "Session" tab and click on "Options for In-Meeting (Basic)", and confirm that Nonverbal Input is activated.

4. If the configuration is disabled, click on the "Allow Status Slider".

5. Select "Toggle On" to validate the adjustment while a test dialogue appears.

Sending Invitations to Participants

There seems to be two options: through invitations to schedules, or via your specific email address. If you want to welcome someone into a calendar, you can see links to calendar events, Outlook Schedule, and Yahoo schedule until your session is saved. Conversely, there's a choice to "copy this invitation" next to the "enter URL" link on this tab. Simply clicking upon that page element will pull up the display with all the crucial facts needed for the conference, such as the URL, which already includes the conference ID. Copy this to your keyboard, open your email app, paste the information into a short email, and get away with it. But, in brief, all members need the conference Address, time and date, and, if necessary, a code.

If you want to check out the functionality before getting other people in, prepare the test conference at this point and click "Start this meeting."

Moreover, inside the first section of the Zoom web app, you can do just the same. The first request will ask you to enter machine audio if you are on a Laptop, and will also provide you with the opportunity to test the microphone and speaker. You can decide to go full-screen mode at the upper right-hand side of the conference window.

Zoom Rooms

Zoom Rooms is a much more premium technology kit available as a forty-nine dollars rental a month. Zoom Rooms, is a new choice for company owners who think remote work would be the standard for the near future. It incorporates audio sessions, web conferencing, and portable video streaming. A Desktop operating Zoom Rooms is the necessary minimum prerequisite, but it is possible to include all smartphones, TV screens, multiple objects, microphones, and cameras into one room. In the Zoom Update Center, you will find the Rooms App and Controller applications.

Polling

The seminar polling functionality helps you to create multiple simultaneous option polling queries for your sessions. At your conference, you will be able to open the questionnaire and collect the answers from your attendees. You will have the option of uploading a polling paper after the conference. Polls can also be administered secretly if you do not want to gather information about the voters with the poll's outcome.

To allow all participants of your company to have the polling function:

1. Log in as an operator to the Zoom web application with the right to change account restrictions.

2. Select "Identity Management" and then "Identity Preferences" in the main navigation.

3. Navigate to the Meetings tab polling alternative and check to allow configuration.

4. If the feature is deactivated, press the trigger "Switch".

5. Select "Switch On" to validate the adjustment while a test dialogue appears.

Polling for your purposes allows:

1. Log in to the website for the Zoom.

2. Click on "Account Management".

3. Click on "Account Settings".

4. Move to the "Conference tab Polling Alternative" and check to allow configuration.

5. If the feature is deactivated, press the trigger option.

6. Select "Switch On" to validate the adjustment while a test dialogue appears.

To generate a poll;

1. Go to the "Meetings" tab, and click on your meeting list. When you do not have a meeting arranged, book a meeting.

2. Look at the bottom of the meeting management section to find the "Poll" alternative. Click on "Add" to start creating the poll.

3. Type in your title and the first query.

4. Write the responses to your question and press the "Save" button below.

5. If you want to attach a new query to the specific survey, press "Attach a Query" to build a new survey.

6. If you repeat the second phase, you will add further polling.

Managing Breakout Rooms

Breakout rooms encourage you to divide up to fifty different sessions of your Zoom Group. The conference host can decide to manually or automatically partition the attendees into other specific sessions and move between meetings. One can also pre-assign breakout room to members before planning the conference instead of handling them after the conference.

1. Begin a meeting, immediately or on time.

2. Select "Rooms to Breakout".

3. Pick the number of rooms you want to build, and how you want to delegate the rooms to your attendees:

   - **Automatically:** let Zoom divide the attendees equally into each room.

   - **Manually:** Pick the participants in each room that you would like.

4. Select "Build Rooms to Breakout".

After the breakout rooms have been built, press "Options" to access additional room choices. Additional choices include;

- Automatically transfer all attendees to breakout rooms: testing this method would automatically move all attendees to breakout rooms. If this method is unmarked, you will need to press "Join to connect" to the breakout space.

- After selected minutes, the breakout rooms close immediately: If this option is verified, the breakout rooms may end immediately after the set time.

- Inform me whenever the time is up: If this choice is tested, inform the host whenever the space breakout time is up.

- Enable attendees to move to the entire phase at any time: If this option is tested, from their conference settings, the participants will switch back to the main session. If this is disabled, they will have to wait until the host finishes the breakout quarters.

Annotation Tools on a Shared Screen

Meeting attendees can annotate as an observer and the one who started sharing their display, on an accessed display. You could also use annotation tools while connecting a whiteboard or when displaying it. The conference host can disable the attendance annotation. If you do not have the annotation choice, assure that the presenter has not disabled the annotation. To permit annotation including all account holders:

1. Log in to the website Zoom

2. Tap on "Account Management" after which "Account Settings" in the top navigation bar will appear.

3. Press on the button to handle.

4. Check for "Activated Annotation" under the conference (simple).

5. If the configuration is deactivated, tap the enable switch. Tap "Turn On" to validate the transition if an authentication dialogue is displayed.

6. Press the box to check to save annotations of accessed screens.

7. Tap the checkbox to limit annotation to material that is shared by the user only.

8. If you just want all participants in your account to allow this setting compulsory, press the lock icon and afterward tap "Lock" to verify the configuration.

Screen annotation for your purposes allows:

1. Log in to the website for the Zoom.

2. Select setups on the "Navigation" panel.

3. Press on the button of "Meetings".

4. Check for "Activated Annotation" under the conference (simple).

5. If the configuration is deactivated, tap the enable switch. Tap "Turn On" to validate the transition if an authentication dialogue is displayed.

6. Press the box to check to save annotations of accessed screens.

7. Tap the checkbox to limit annotation to material that is shared by the user only.

8. If you just want to allow this setting compulsory, press the lock icon and afterward tap "Lock" to verify the configuration.

You will see those tools for annotation:

- **Mouse:** Turn off annotation toolkits and turn to a mouse cursor. If annotation tools are disabled, this icon will be blue.

- **Note:** Pick the previous rectangular or loop icon to add a transparent block or loop to underline an accessed screen and whiteboard area.

- **Stamp:** add clearly defined icons such as a star or check the label.

- **Spotlight/Arrow:** Turn the mouse to arrow or limelight.

- **Select** (only accessible when accessed screen or whiteboard is launched): Pick, start moving, or reformat your annotations. Tap and hold your mouse to show a choice area for selecting multiple annotations simultaneously.

- **Text:** Font in.

- **Draw:** Put lines, dots, and patterns in it.

- **Undo:** Do away with your recent annotation.

- **Redo:** Redo the most recent annotation you have undone.

- **Eraser:** Tap and push to delete the annotation.

- **Format:** Modify annotation tool configuration options such as color, line width, and icons.

- **Clear:** Withdraw all annotations.

- **Save:** Secure provided screen/whiteboard, and "Gif file" or "Printout" annotations. The documents are created to the local location of the playback.

Sharing a Whiteboard

The whiteboard tool will enable you to show a whiteboard that you and certain attendees can annotate on it if permitted. To start whiteboard:

1. Tap "Share Screen" after you have entered the conference

2. Activate "Whiteboard" and tap "Screen Share".

3. The annotation instruments would become accessible when you press on the "Whiteboard".

4. The Whiteboard can be saved as a "File" type. It will then be processed as "whiteboard.png" in the Zoom file.

If you already have display sharing on sequentially, numerous participants will be able to present a whiteboard simultaneously.

However, you will have a double screen allowed to see two whiteboards in one go, even your whiteboard, and some other whiteboard.

Zoom Phone

Zoom Phone is a straightforward and easy cloud requesting solution designed for Zoom customers who wish to set up video-free quick calls. If you are not using an in-depth conference, you had usually turned to zoom; conversely, you can initiate a speedy VoIP request using the same techniques you already love. The Zoom Phone entity separates Zoom into a fully functional collaboration and communication item, in the same way that is comprehensive with voice, conference, texting, and video. Zoom Phone gives:

- Smart call maintenance and forwarding so that you will never miss a crucial discussion.

- State-of-the-art software for desktop and mobile computer systems alike.

- Tools for automatic assistant and Interactive voice to transfer the correct decisions to the most configured agents.

- Call capturing and text messages so you can pay attention to discussions quickly or read transcripts on any phone system, computer, or mobile device.

- High definition audio protects detailed discussions that do not affect comfort.

1.6 Zoom Security Issues and Updates

Recently a variety of questions have been raised about Zoom; both in terms of protection and conflicts with unwelcome visitors identified as Zoom-bombers.

The organization has made numerous efforts to address these concerns and has convinced the consumers that security and privacy are relevant. This involves essential items, including deleting the meeting ID from the call's title bar or people's posted web-photos of the meeting, they would not be revealed to potential misuse. The firm has issued several changes to the software to improve security credibility.

Zoom-Bombers

Zoom's growth in popularity would cause the service to be exploited by internet bullies and individuals who have so much time on their hands. Some people have been tracking down public and illegal Zoom meetings and letting themselves in, then "bombing" with explicit images, pornography, and other objectionable material on the line. There are numerous ways you can keep it from happening, including protecting your calls, blocking screen sharing, and even stopping footage. Also, the team behind Zoom continually makes changes to cover your needs and keep them secured.

Default Security Updates

To further inform consumers, the Zoom has been revised with some security improvements. All of them are the provision for Zoom meetings to have a password as usual. Combined with simulated waiting rooms, this means that only specific individuals who have been asked to the call can be invited in reality. Another move is ensuring that calls are confidential and stable.

Zoom Security Tools

Zoom also has made it easier to schedule your conferences and to protect them as they occur. There are a lot of security options that you can now use with a few taps, including the option to secure the meeting as it begins so that no other members can participate, delete current call members, change attendees, and even disable private conversation. To use the Zoom protection features, you can either press the protection button that shows in the browser when the call happens or swings over a person to connect with them directly-for example, to delete them from the call.

Reporting Other Participants

It is now possible to respond to the call to all people who are not invited or cause problems. You should also submit a note to the Zoom Confidence and security committee to tackle device abuse and eliminate them from the call. In the future, this would effectively block them from the service. To do this, click on the "Conference Seat" button and then press "Record".

Chapter 2: Setting Up the Zoom App

With more individuals beginning to work in most industries from home, mobile video conference technology has never been more relevant. Resources such as Zoom, which provides remote meetings and video calls, become more critical than ever to help keep companies going smoothly when traditional offices are locked. Fortunately, downloading Zoom to the Computer and Smartphone is a quick procedure that will get you running smoothly in just a few moments with the system. Although you will need to sign up for a new plan to use Zoom, you will do it straight away once the software is enabled on your device.

Downloading and Installing Zoom on Computer

1. Enable the internet browser on your device and link it to the zoom.us homepage.

2. Look at the bottom of the list, and in the header of the website page, click "Open".

3. Click "Open" on the "Application Center" page under the segment labeled "Zoom Application for Conferences".

4. Then the Zoom application begins installing.

5. To launch the installation, you can then press on the ".exe link".

6. When enabled, you will need to sign into the Zoom profile that can be established via the Zoom page if you do not have another one. If developed, you can use Zoom to fulfill all your video conferencing and digital needs as usual.

Downloading and Installing Zoom on Smartphones

1. Press on the "Application Store".

2. Tap "Applications" in the Play Store.

3. Click the "Searching icon" found at the top left of the app store application.

4. Enter zoom in the text field of the search, then press "Zoom Web Conferences" from the search list.

5. Tap "Download" on the next page.

6. Tap "Agree" in the next tab.

7. If you have enabled Zoom, click "Open".

2.1 Getting Started on Windows and Mac

Zoom combines cloud video communications, quick online conferences, and easy-to-use social networking under one application. Their technology delivers the best functionality in audio, video, and remote display sharing throughout various channels.

Select "Enter a Meeting" after the Zoom starts to enter a conference without logging in. Select "Sign In" if you wish to register in and launch or plan your conference. Try using your Facebook, Google, or Zoom credentials to log in. Select "Sign in free" if you are not using a profile.

Home

If you do have a profile with Zoom but are unable to recall your name, press "Forget". You could see the "Home" tab when logging in, where you can press on certain choices:

- **New Conference**: Launch a conference right away. For immediate conferences, drop-down menu to allow video, or use the private session ID.

- **Join:** Attend a conference.

- **Schedule:** arrange an upcoming meeting.

- **Share Screen:** Share your display by entering the shared key or conference ID in a Zoom Space.

- **Time and date with profile picture:** Swipe over the photo to adjust the background photo and press on the camera button.

- **Upcoming:** Shows the present-day next conference. If you want to schedule future events, install a third-party scheduling program.

For these choices, click on your profile image.

- Configurations: Use configurations in the app which you can alter.

Settings

General

Video

Audio

Share Screen

Chat

Background & Filters

Recording

Profile

Statistics

Keyboard Shortcuts

Accessibility

☑ Enter full screen when a participant shares screen

☐ Maximize Zoom window when a participant share screen

☑ Scale to fit shared content to Zoom window

☐ Enable the remote control of all applications

☐ Side-by-side mode

☑ Silence system notifications when sharing desktop

- Adjust your status to "Open", "Do Not Interrupt", or "down".

- My Profile: To change your portfolio, open the website Zoom.

- Support: The Zoom Aid Center unlocks.

- Check for Updates: Check to see if the Zoom is correct.

- Around Zoom: See the previous edition.

- Move to Profile View: If you want a smaller display, adjust the Zoom slider to profile view.

- Sign Up.

- Update to Pro.

Chat

To access private messages with your friends or group conversations, click the "Chat" key. These functions can be found in the left-hand panel:

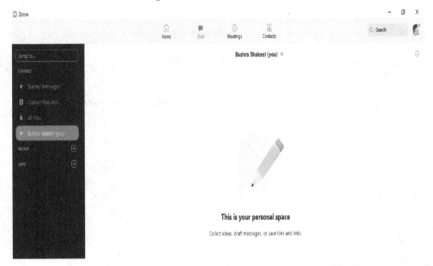

- **Move to the checkbox:** Check for a network or a communication.

- **Starred texts:** Open messages that you have starred at.

- To use your private chat room, tap on your title.

- **Insert icon:** Launch a new conversation with one of your friends, set up a community conversation channel, or enter an established channel.

- Tap on a link under "Recent" to see the conversation history and begin talking with them. Connections have a progress icon in front of the name.

- You may use certain functions in the chat window after picking a link or channel in the left-hand panel:

- **Star icon:** attach the person or network to your starred folder, allowing easy access to the connections or networks.

- **Video icon:** Launch a contact call. If a channel is chosen, it will initiate a meeting of all channel participants.

- **New screen icon** (override your link or network name to view this icon): Activates the conversation you chose in a new browser.

- **Text Box:** Compile texts and send them to your interaction or site. You can submit screenshots, images, fragments of code, including animated images, too.

Phone

- Click the "Phones tab" to make and receive calls, display the conversation background, and use "Zoom Screen" to play voice messages.

- History tab: Access and delete records and history of the call.

- Voice and video tab: Perform and handle messages to voicemail.

- Dial pad: Make several calls by inserting a mobile number automatically or by browsing through the numbers.

Meetings

- To access, start, update, and uninstall scheduled meetings, pick the conferences tab, and then click "around".

- After you pick a planned meeting in the left-hand column, you can tap on the various choices:

- **Icon to add:** Hold a news conference.

- Check icon: if you do not see your conference planned, check the conference list.

- **Launch:** Launch the planned meeting you have chosen for your next appointments.

- **Copy Invitation:** Save the invitation text of the planned meeting to automatically insert it into a file, instant messaging, etc. If you want to see the email you are copying, press "Display Meeting Email".

- **Update:** Update your planned meeting session choices.

Contacts

- To access and track your notifications, click on the contact information tab.

- **Folder tab:** Open a list of all your connections, including links with highlighted, default, and auto-replies. If you have Zoom Rooms at your company, you can also find a list of Zoom Rooms.

- **Tab Networks:** Open the channels list (used for social messaging). Starred networks will be on the top of the list feature.

- **Icon Add:** Show interaction and channel choices. You may add an email, create a community of contacts, create a server, or enter a server.

In-Meeting Controls

You can access the session settings found at the bottom of the conference window after you have begun or entered a conference (keep moving your cursor in the Zoom browser to view session controls).

2.2 Getting Started on Smartphones/Mobile Devices

There are several settings you need to do while setting up Zoom on your smartphones.

Using Android Fingerprint Authentication

If you have a fingerprint reader on your Android smartphone, you can activate fingerprint recognition, enabling you to log in to the Zoom with the finger easily. You need to include your fingerprint in your Phone settings before using the fingerprint recognition in the iOS Zoom application. If you've already inserted your fingerprint, move to the segment below. In Android 9.0, these measures apply. These steps can vary, based on the device of your unit. If this move does not function for you, please visit the help site for guidance from your supplier to verify fingerprints.

1. Navigate to "Configuration".
2. Click "Position and Security".
3. Tap "Fingerprints" in the "Computer Protection line".
4. Tap "establish" then follow the fingerprints on-screen directions. For better flexibility, you might want to add more than one fingerprint.

To enable fingerprint in Zoom, follow these steps:

1. Select "Settings".
2. To access your profile configurations, press on your "title".
3. To activate this, press the "Use Fingerprint Identification" button.
4. Then you can sign in with your fingerprint.

To enable fingerprint while sign into Zoom and follow these steps:

1. Sign in to the "Zoom."

2. A pop-up window will appear asking you to log in with the "Fingerprint Code".

3. To allow fingerprint scanner, click "Yes".

4. Now you can log in with your fingerprint.

To use fingerprints, follow these steps:

When you sign in with the Mobile Zoom application each time, you will see the corresponding message asking you to sign in with your fingerprint. Position your finger on the fingerprint scanner on your mobile. If your computer fails to remember your fingerprints after three trials, you must use your login and password to log in to the Zoom.

Using Siri with Zoom

The iOS application Zoom involves executing some actions utilizing Siri. In the Zoom application, you can establish Siri shortcuts, which will enable you to enter the next meeting appointment, see important meetings, or begin the private discussion. You can also launch a video conference in Zoom without establishing a Siri shortcut with a touch.

To add Zoom shortcuts to Siri, follow these methods:

1. Enable the iOS device's Zoom Program, and press "Configurations".

2. Click "Shortcuts" on Siri.

3. Pick the shortcut you want to use and press "Use to Siri".

4. To capture audio for a shortcut, press the red recording tab.

5. To save the captured sound, press "Finished".

To perform a Zoom action with Siri, follow these steps:

1. Tell "Hey Siri, phone Zoom (Zoom user number)" to facilitate a video conference with that communication.

2. You will say, "Hey Siri," accompanied by the terms you have selected to execute certain acts as you set up the other passwords.

3. You may also send Siri guidance by keeping down the final key on an iPhone 8 and older versions or pressing and holding an iPhone 10 start button.

4. You do not need to establish a shortcut to dial Siri for a Zoom touch.

Getting Started with iOS

You can attend groups, chat with friends, and open a contact list using the Zoom Cloud Groups software on iOS.

1. Sign in and Join

To use all the functions, open the Zoom application, and log in to your profile. You will also attend a meeting without logging in. If you enter without logging in, press on the download button to activate simple session configurations.

2. Meet and Chat

Click Meeting and Communicate for these conference functionalities after signing in:

- **New Conference:** Launch a conference immediately using your meeting ID or new conference ID.

- **Enter:** Join a group using the conference name.

- **Schedule:** Organize a one-time or periodic conference.

- **Share Screen:** Insert a Shared Key or ID to display your computer screen in a Zoom application.

- To use your chat room, add your Password.

You can access the following functions of chat, too:

- **More icon**: Launch a one-on-one communication conversation.

- **Star icon:** Open your star connections and networks and start a conversation.

3. **Phone**

   - Tap Mobile to use the functionality of a Zoom Screen.

   - Permission is required for the Zoom handset.

   - **Keypad tab:** Use your phone number or business number to call or communicate.

   - **History tab:** List the received, missing, and reported calls in your call log.

   - **Voice message tab:** Play and uninstall messages to voicemail.

4. **Meetings**

   - **Start:** Use your meeting ID to launch an instant session or a meeting you have arranged

   - **Send Invitation:** Invite others through text message to your meeting ID, email, copy the specifics of the conference, and then paste them into a calendar request.

   - **Edit:** Update your meeting ID Settings

To view, update, begin, enter, or cancel the scheduled meeting:

   - You can add, begin, or remove conferences only if you are the host.

5. **Contacts**

   - Tap Connections to list all connections you have, and introduce new ones.

- **Group tab:** To launch a one-on-one conversation with someone, click "contacts".

- **Tab Networks:** Open a list of highlighted networks, both common and personal.

- **Places tab:** Open the Zoom Rooms list. To begin a conference with it, click a "Zoom Room".

- **Plus (+) icon:** Add a customized touch, enter or build a new community chat service, or add a Zoom Market application.

6. **Settings**

   - Tap configurations to view the setup for meetings and chat.

   - Tap your username to change the graphic, the name, and the code of your account.

   - **Conferences:** Change settings once you start a conference to enable/disable your speaker, voice, or photo;

   - **Contacts:** identify contacts by phone utilizing Zoom, and accept requests for communications.

   - **Messages:** Allow or disable the preview of interactions in conversations.

   - **Notifications:** Adjust when new messages are alerted to you by Zoom

   - **Telephone** (only available if you have Zoom Telephone): Display your business number and specific screen number.

   - **General:** Activate/deactivate built-in call or blur screenshot on any task.

   - **About:** Open a version of the software and provide reviews.

2.3 Signing Up and Activation on Windows

This fast start guide will introduce you to your new Zoom profile, including important steps such as arranging your first conference, uploading your Zoom application, and upgrading your Zoom account.

Join Existing Account

If you are connected to an already existing account, Zoom will send you an email. Press on Enable Your Zoom Account after you obtain this notification.

Creating a New Account

1. You can continue by adding your email address or heading to http:/zoom.us/ and signing up with a free account.

2. Tap the Zoom email to activate.

3. Fill out your email and Password in the section.

4. When you have an email linked with Zoom, click https:/zoom.us/download the Zoom software here.

Sign in to Zoom

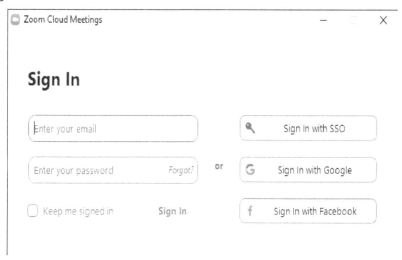

1. Go to Zoom sign-in page with the link zoom.us/sign in.

2. It will ask you about your email address and your Password for Zoom.

3. Fill in the tabs and click on "Sign In".

4. You can stay signed in longer on your Zoom account by clicking on "Stay Signed In" on the page.

Customize your Profile

The Zoom profile helps you modify your user credentials, including your title, Password, email account, etc. This data appears in the database to other people, such as the title, agency, and job description.

Log in to the Zoom website to view your Zoom account and choose preview. You can see and modify the configurations below:

- **Profile Photo:** Press Update to add or remove your profile photo, fix the crop area on your existing one, or download a different one. You can also remove the photo from your account by clicking Remove.

- **Name:** To change your username, right-click on Delete. Other profile details can also be added, including Department, Work Description, Business, and Location.

- In the Zoom desktop app, your screen photo, name, number, agency, work description, and position will be shown to other users as they swipe over your profile.

- **Phone number**: The contact information added to your account is permanent. If you enter an internal number, you will be asked by Zoom to validate it before it shows in your account.

- **Account Number:** It mentions your account details under your title. You should remember this if you request help in Zoom assistance, as it will allow you to find your account more easily.

- **Personal conference ID:** Use your private conference ID for quick conferences, click "Edit" on the right-hand side to update your specific meeting ID or verify the function.

- **Personal Link:** You can set up a private link if you have a paying license on a Company or Educational account. Select "Setting" or modifying your current "Personal Connection" to the right.

- **Sign-In Account:** Press Edit to modify the username and Password you used to log in on the right-hand page. Know more about modifying your email if you do not have the edit feature or extra guidance.

- **User Class and characteristics:** Shows the license type and add-ons that you are allocated to. To know more about each license or functionality, press the question mark?).

- **Capacity:** Demonstrates your ability to reach and conduct webinar (if possible). You will need to buy and grant multiple licenses to alter this.

- **Local organization:** Displays the community classes to which your account holder or administrator has delegated you.

- **Language:** Press "Edit" to adjust the current Zoom online portal script.

- **Date and Time:** Change the local date, time format, and date format by pressing "Edit".

- **Note:** This setting can also be utilized by Zoom Phone if you have a Zoom Phone license. Be sure you choose the proper time zone as it will impact the background of the call, transcripts, text message, and operating hours.

- **Connectivity of Calendar and Contacts:** Press "Link to Calendar and Contact System" to begin merging your Google, Office 365, or sharing contacts with Zoom.

- **Sign-in Account:** Click on "Change" to modify your username address.

- Host Key: To reveal your hosting key, press "Display and Edit" to adjust your host key.

- **Signed-In software:** Press "Sign Me Off" from All Accounts to sign up on mobile accounts and laptop. After logging off, you will need to reset your Password to earlier versions of Zoom. This can be helpful if a computer that has Zoom enabled and signed in is lost.

2.4 Scheduling a Meeting

Zoom provides many means of arranging a conference. A host retains power over the configurations for his planned events, except settings that an admin requires to be installed in the account for all accounts or all members of that group.

- Schedule from the Web Computer or Smartphone App

- Schedule from the web browser Zoom

- Schedule with PDF Administrative Assistants Manuals (Outlook, Google)

To schedule a meeting on Windows or Mac.

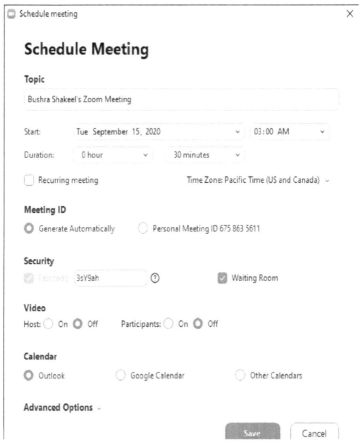

1. Open the account with the Zoom and sign up to preview.

2. Tap on the button for "Schedule".

3. This would open a window in the planner.

4. Pick your preferences for the conference. Notice that any of these alternatives will not be accessible if they have been removed and restricted to the role's account or community level.

   • **Subject:** Add a theme for your conference, or name.

- **Start:** Pick the time and date you wish to meet. You can begin your conference before the planned schedule at any moment. You can still step in at any time automatically. For example, in the area of minutes, you can enter fifteen to plan a period in fifteen minutes.

- **Time Zone:** Zoom can use the time zone of your device, by default. To pick a single standard time, press on the drop-down menu.

- **Repeated meeting:** Pick whether you would like to have a recurring meeting (for each conference, the conference ID will stay the same).

5. **Communication ID**

   - **Quick Create:** Create a special random conference tab.

   - **Specific Assembly Code:** Use the "Own Assembly" Key.

6. **Security**

   - **Confirmation code:** Insert passwords from the conference. You would be asked to submit this to the participants before attending your planned meeting.

   - **Note:** The passwords for the conference must satisfy the difficulty criteria defined by the administrator.

   - Waiting Room: Activate the waiting room to wait.

7. **Video**

   - **Host:** Pick if you like a screenshot of the webserver on or off as you start the conference. The presenter will have the opportunity to resume his recording even though you want to off.

- **Participants:** Pick if you like clips of the attendees on or off when you start the group. The respondents would still have the chance to begin their recording, even if you want to off.

8. **Audio:** Enable users to connect using Smartphone only, Device Sound just, anything, or third parties Audio (if your profile is selected).

9. **Calendar:** To attach the conference to a calendar system and to give invitations to the attendees.

10. **Outlook:** Open the desktop application for Outlook, and establish a meeting schedule.

    - By using a Windows app, you will see Outlook.

    - If you are using a Mac OS, you can see iCal.

11. **Google Calendar:** Open the standard web browser calendar, and build a meeting schedule.

12. **Other Calendars:** Open the new tab where the conference's text can be replicated or edited into the desired mode of communication for the individual. You can also download a File type that most email programs can access.

13. **Advanced Choices:** To see more meeting choices press on the button.

    - **Require host to participate:** Encourage members to attend the conference without you or before joining. The session will end for Simple (free) users after forty minutes if three or more people to attend the meeting.

    - **Mute attendees on the entrance:** This will silence attendees when they enter the conference if they cannot participate before the moderator. After entering the session, the members will un-mute themselves.

- **Only approved users can participate**: limit the conference access such that only sign-in user can participate.

- **Record session manually:** Choose what you want to capture remotely (to your desktop) or in the database. This requires additional areas with cloud services for the conference.

- **Plan for**: If you have a participant's planning rights, you can select the one you want to plan for, from the drop-down section.

- **Alternate hosts:** insert the email account of some other authorized Zoom person on your profile to enter them in to start the conference.

- **Interpretation** (only assisted by Mac and Windows employees): allow assembly language translation.

14. Select "Save" to stop, and reopen the scheduling service you chose to add the conference. If you are arranging a periodic activity, your calendar service's repetition would have to be calculated. Selecting "Other Calendars" would enable you to copy/paste the planned details such as time, date, and URL.

2.5 Joining a Meeting

You can install the Zoom application from the Download Center while attending a video conference on a smartphone or computer. Alternatively, when you press a join page, you will be asked to download and activate Zoom. You can even attend a "Test Conference" to get to know Zoom. The conference has a specific nine, ten, or eleven-digit number, called a session ID, to access a video conference. If you are attending via smartphone, the teleconference number included in the invitation will be needed.

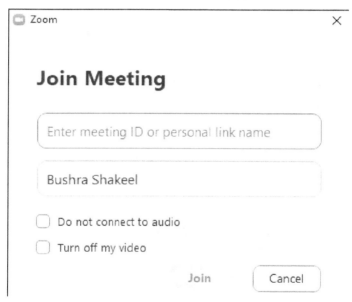

On Windows and Mac

Enable the web app for zoom. Enter a conference using one of the following methods:

1. If you wish to enter without logging in, click "Attend a Conference."

2. Log in to Zoom, and then press "Enter."

3. Insert the ID number for the conference and the name for the show.

4. When you log in, change your Password when you do not want to use your default configuration.

5. If you are not logged in, type a name for the window.

6. Check whether you want an audio and/or video link and press "Enter."

On Linux

Enable the web app for zoom. Enter a conference using one of the following methods:

1. If you want to join while logging in, click "Attend a Meeting".

2. Log in to Zoom, and then press "Enter."

3. Enter the Identification number and name of the conference.

4. When you log in, change your Password when you do not want to use your default configuration.

5. If you are not logged in, type a name for the show.

6. Check whether you want an audio and/or video link and press "Enter".

On Android

Open the mobile application to zoom in. If you haven't yet downloaded the Android Zoom application, you can install it from the play store. Enter a conference using one of the following methods:

1. If you wish to enter without logging in, tap "Attend a Meeting".

2. Log in to Zoom and then press "Enter."

3. Insert the identification number for the conference and the title for the screen.

4. When you log in, change your Password when you do not want to use your default configuration.

5. If you are not logged in, type a name for the screen.

6. Select if you want to link Audio and/or video, and tap "Enter Meeting".

On iOS

Open the phone application to zoom in. If you haven't already downloaded the Phone Zoom application, you can install it from the Application Store. Enter a conference using one of the following methods:

1. If you want to enter without logging in, tap "Attend a Meeting."

2. Log in to Zoom and then press "Enter."

3. Insert the Identification number for the conference and the name for the screen.

4. When you log in, change your Password when you do not want to use your default configuration.

5. If you are not logged in, type a name for the screen.

6. Choose if you want to link Audio and/or video, and click "Enter."

From Web Browser

To join a meeting from Google Chrome, follow these steps:

1. Start Chrome.

2. Go over to "join.zoom.us".

3. Join the presenter/organizer with your conference name.

4. Tap "Join".

5. If it is the first time from Chrome to join a meeting, you will be asked to open the Zoom application to attend the conference.

6. In the corresponding application, you should check "Always allow these kinds of connections to skip this step in forward".

7. Select "Open Zoom Meets (PC)" or "Activate" zoom.us (Mac) icon.

To join a meeting from the Safari Browser, follow these steps:

1. Start Safari.

2. Go over to "join.zoom.us".

3. Join the host/organizer with your conference name.

4. Tap to that to "Enter" a meeting.

5. Select "Enable" when asked if you wish to access zoom.us.

To join a meeting from Internet Explorer, follow these steps:

1. Enable "Edge" or "Internet Explorers".

2. Go over to "join.zoom.us".

3. Join the host/organizer with your conference ID.

4. Tap to "Enter".

To join a meeting from Mozilla Firefox, follow these steps:

1. Start Firefox.

2. Go over to "join.zoom.us".

3. Join the host/organizer with your session ID.

4. Tap "Enter".

5. If this is your first experience entering Firefox, you could produce the Zoom kit or the Zoom launcher.

6. To miss this step in the future, look for zoommtg ties in "Note my Preference".

7. Click On "Connect".

Through Email

1. In your address or schedule invitations, press the link to join.

2. You can be asked to open the Zoom, based on the preferred internet browser.

Through Messaging

If you are connected with the Zoom web software or smartphone app, others will be able to give you an invitation for a meeting through instant messaging. You will get an incoming message confirmation showing the name and a ringtone who are requesting. Click "Agree" to join the individual who is inviting you to the conference.

Through Telephone

On your cell, call the number given in your invitation to teleconferences. When asked, input the conference identification number using your dial pad. You will have the authority to expand your two-digit user ID to be correlated with your desktop if you have already entered the conference over a desktop. If you haven't entered your screen, simply click # once again when asked to enter your name.

Through IP Address

In the application to meetings, tap the IP address you got. Enter the contact identifier via touching tones followed with #. Or you could just use dial sequences to explicitly access the session, such as 191.160.11.55#010111000.

2.6 Starting a Meeting

If you are the conference organizer and wish to initiate or attend a planned meeting; there are many ways you can participate. For Mac, Laptop, or Linux, the Zoom application for iOS or Android, the web server, or an H.323 or SIP system, you can launch the conference from the Zoom desktop application as host. Using your hosting key, you can initiate a conference by phone as the moderator.

From Windows or Mac

1. Tap Conferences in the Zoom application.

2. Pick the conference you want to launch under the tab "Below".

3. Show up additional choices.

4. Click the "Start" button.

From Linux

1. Tap "Conferences" in the Zoom application.

2. Under "Incoming", swing over the conference you wish to continue.

3. Show up additional choices.

4. Click the "Start" button.

From Android/iOS

1. Tap "Forward" in the smartphone Zoom application.

2. Select "Begin" next to the conference you want to begin.

From Web Browser

1. Go to "My conferences".

2. Click on "start" next to the conference you want to open under the "Pending Sessions" tab.

3. To begin the conference, the Zoom client must start manually.

From Email or Calendar

1. Verify that you are logging in to the same account at zoom.us/profile.

2. Begin the conference by selecting the "URL Connect" in your invitations to an email or schedule.

3. Zoom client can boot and resume the conference manually.

From the IP Address

You will need to use the keypad string's host button to initiate a conference as the host with an H.323 or SIP system. See zoom.us/profile to find the host address.

2.7 Setting up Zoom Webinars

Zoom Webinar enables you to show up to ten thousand view-only participants of a Zoom conference, based on the extent of your webinar certificate. Webinar licenses begin at a capacity of hundred participants and have a level of up to ten-thousands. You can share your computer, video, and Audio as the moderator or panel member in a webinar. Guests can use the talk or questionnaire tools to connect with the moderator and panel members.

Webinars can develop effective-registration, with the option to apply personalized registration queries to the moderator, or registering may be shut off at the webinar by simply pressing on a link. Webinars may be conducted once, reoccur in a sequence, or held several times in the same meeting.

Registration for Webinars

Webinars may require pre-registration before the activity. The host may either accept all registered members immediately or accept them individually. The host will ask questions about customized confirmation and remove the registration files. Conversely, the webinar access may be switched off by the host. Upon entering, the attendees will also be asked to type their phone number and email address, and the records will be restricted to this. There are several webinar clearance processes, which require registration

- **Approve immediately-** All webinar registrants will immediately receive an email confirmation containing information on how to access the webinar.

- **Manually Accept-** The Webinar host may manually allow or deny the consent of a registrant. If a registered owner is accepted, an email with instructions about accessing the webinar will be sent to them.

Scheduling a Webinar with Registration

Scheduling a validation webinar demands that your registrants fill out a short questionnaire before obtaining the invitation to access your webinar. This helps you to compile the enrollees' names, email addresses as well as other data. You may decide to manually approve someone who signs or accepts participants by hand. If you do not need to compile details about registrants, you can arrange a registration-free webinar. If you plan a continuing registration webinar, modifying the repeating webinar will result in missing registration records, implying attendees will need to register again.

To Schedule a registered webinar, follow these steps:

1. Log in to the website for the Zoom.
2. Select "Webinars".

3. A list of planned webinars you will see.

4. Pick a "Webinar" to "Plan".

5. Choose the webinar configuration you like.

6. To seek registration, pick the "Login" method. When registration is needed, and the webinar is a regular occurrence, choose one of the choices below:

   • Attendees enroll once and can join all of the events: attendees can join all the activities. The session will list all times and dates, and the registered owner will be reported for all events.

   • Participants must register to participate for each event: Registrants must register individually for each event to participate. On the recipient tab, they may pick only one time and date.

   • Attendees enroll once and then choose to join one or more events: Registrants register automatically and choose to join any or even more events. They will get to pick the times and occasions they choose to participate and will only be reported. They have several choices to pick from.

7. Select "Schedule".

To set automatic registration approval, follow these steps:

1. Prepare for your webinar.

2. To access the registration choices under "Invite Guests," drop straight to the bottom of the "Webinar Information Tab".

3. It will display "Approval Automatically" or "Approval Manually" beside "Approval".

4. If it lists "Authorize Manually", right-click on "Delete".

5. Choose "Accept Automatically".

6. Select "Save."

7. Copy the Link for login or an invite to discuss it with your attendants.

To set manual registration approval, follow these steps:

1. Prepare for your webinar.

2. To access the registration choices under "Invite Guests," drop straight to the bottom of the "Webinar Information Tab".

3. It will display "Approval Automatically" or "Approval Manually" beside "Approval".

4. If it lists "Authorize Automatically", right-click on "Delete".

5. Choose "Accept Manually".

6. Select "Save".

7. Copy the Link for login or an invite to discuss it with your attendants.

8. Go to the Webinars page after a participant has enrolled.

9. To display the information, tap on the title of the webinar.

10. To "Handle Participants" right, click "Delete".

11. Choose the user(s) you want to accept and/or refuse. If accepted, they will provide an email about how to access the webinar.

Scheduling a Webinar without Registration

Organizing a webinar before registration would enable participants to participate without having to pre-register.

Attendees are expected to input their email address and phone number upon entering. Conversely, you should arrange a webinar to obtain more details for admission.

To schedule a webinar without registration, follow these steps:

1. Log in to the website for the Zoom.

2. Webinars Press. The list of planned webinars can be found here.

3. Pick a Webinar to Plan.

4. Choose the webinar configuration you like.

- **Subject:** Pick your webinar theme/title.

- **Definition:** Enter an appropriate overview of the webinar. This will appear on your registration form.

- **Use a template:** If you have built webinar models before, you can pick one of them to add to this latest webinar.

- **Time:** Pick your webinar time and date.

- **Duration:** Pick the estimated webinar time. Notice that this is for planning purposes only. After this period, the webinar would not finish.

- **Time Zone:** Zoom can use the local time you assigned to your Account by definition. To pick a local time zone, press Dropdown.

- **Periodic webinar:** Verify if you would like a periodic webinar, i.e., for each conference, the conference ID would stay the same. That would open up new opportunities for recurrence.

- **Webinar Passcode:** Verify here if attendees are expected to enter a password to access your webinar, and change the security code expected. Participants would be asked to enter the passwords before entering your webinar if they join automatically. It is included in the confirmation email of enrollment, and if they access by tapping on the links in this file, they do not need to enter the passwords.

- **Video:** Pick whether video may or may not be allowed during the webinar.

- **Data:** Select whether to permit telephone-only, software-only data, telephone and machine audio (both), or third-party Audio (if allowed to access your account).

- **Plan With:** If you have some user's planning right, you can select from the left column, the one you want to plan with. You must also be a Registered User and have a webinar license.

- **Alternative Hosts:** Insert the email account of another authorized Zoom person on your profile to enable you in the absence to begin the conference.

5. Select "Schedule".

6. Your webinar is set for now. You will copy the connect link or the application to share it with your attendants under Inviting participants.

Starting a Webinar

There are some ways to get your webinar going.

1. Log in to the online portal of Zoom, and select "Webinars". Look for the webinar, and press "Start".

2. Tap the "Conferences" button in the Zoom application. Look for the webinar, and press "Start".

3. If this has been connected to your calendars, follow the link seen on your calendar notification. Before tapping on the page, please ensure that you are signed in to your Zoom profile.

2.8 Sending Invitation links

There are many options to invite the members to an immediate or planned conference. You may also introduce a room device (requires Cloud Space Connection add-on) by telephone (allows the Audio-Conferencing strategy).

Inviting Others during a Meeting

1. Enable the Zoom Screen Client.

2. Start, join, or enter meetings.

3. Select the "Controls of Meetings Participants".

4. Select "Invite" in the "Attendees" row at the right.

Choose from the choices below:

1. Email

- Tap on the section "Email".

- Pick a "Provider" for Email:

- Default Email: Allow someone to access your device using your current email address.

- Email or Yahoo Mail: Use the Email or Yahoo web portal to notify others. You are asked to log in to your account.

- The conference information will be immediately written with a new email in the email address.

- Add receivers and send the file.

2. Contacts

- Tap on the "Web Contacts" page.

- From the screen, pick their title, or locate an email.

- Tap on the user you want to invite. You can have different contacts. When you do this, your name will be displayed, which will show at the top of the screen in the column.

- Tap "Invite" to the bottom-right corner.

3. **URL**

- Click the "Invitation Link" or "Copy Invite" button to submit details from your quick conference somewhere.

- **Copy Invite Page:** Copy the address connected to the conference.

- **Download Invitation:** Download the entire text of your invitation.

- Using "Ctrl + V" on Computers, or "Cmd +V" on a Mac to paste the URL or invitations. You can also straight-click "Copy" and "Paste" link.

Inviting Others to a Scheduled Meeting

You can also arrange a conference before beginning the session and invite others.

1. **Desktop Client**

- Enable the "Zoom Screen Client".

- Have a meeting planned.

- Select "Conferences".

- Choose the session you want to invite everyone to.

- Tap the "Invitation" to copy.

- The invite to the conference will be replicated, and you can insert the detail into an email or somewhere else you want to send it.

2. **Web Portal**

- Log in to the website for the Zoom.

- Tap "Conferences" in the "Search section".

- Click on "Conference Subject".

- There are ways to add to the calendar beside "Time".

- Clicking on "Yahoo Calendar" or "Google Calendar" would immediately generate a calendar event in the particular email system you pick.

- Clicking on "Outlook Calendar" will create a ".ics" folder that you are importing into your "Outlook Calendar".

- You can also transfer the details to the conference manually by pressing "Transfer Invitation".

- If you choose "Copy Invite", the text of the invitation for meeting will create another tab.

- Select "Invitation" to "Connect" and "copy".

- You can copy and submit the invitation via email, or elsewhere.

Chapter 3: Online Teaching with Zoom App

According to Zoom, the app is the pioneer in digital video networking with a fast, secure cloud network for video and audio chat, interaction, talk, and webinars through smartphones, laptops, telephone lines, and room networks.

Zoom is essentially a collaboration system that allows businesses and individuals to keep in touch with each other through video conferencing capabilities. The method has numerous benefits and strengths. If you are curious that Zoom is right for your teaching, continue reading this Zoom online teaching guide. This interactive communication device links interactive team leaders with powerful audio, video, and collaboration tools. The main aspects of Zooming include High Definition live phone talk, VoIP (Voice over Information Protocol) video conferencing, and quick message, digital backdrops for video calling, sharing the cameras and interactive whiteboards, and hosting webinars on Zoom that can enhance learning experiences of your students.

3.1 Scheduling your Class

To schedule through the Learning Management System (LMS), Zoom provides expanded features and functionality.

1. Sign in to the LMS and visit the outside tool connect Zoom.

2. Select the "Meeting Schedule" tab.

3. Enter Issue, Date, and other relevant information and click "Schedule".

4. Compliance is encouraged before arranging a meeting, as this helps you produce a compliance summary after the meeting has finished.

Basic Practices for Online Class

Log in and remain signed in to the Zoom Web software.

- Test your performance on the phone. You can need to hold your Screen off if you are on the public internet to boost the image.

- Turn on your computer to get an eye-level shot.

- If you worry about reducing background noise, remain quiet.

- Make sure you are seated in a peaceful, well-lit location.

- Aware of what's right around you. Note to get a sturdy wall behind you or switch on the simulated backdrop.

Host an Ad-Hoc Meeting

1. Open your mobile application to zoom in and click "Home".

2. Click the button to "Enter Conference".

3. If you are in the Zoom room, press the "Members" button at the bottom of the page and invite more members.

Teaching Live using Zoom

- Teachers should arrange Zoom sessions and post the links to their digital learning sessions.

- Students and Teachers shall, at the proper time, click on the conference link and administer the class as planned.

Recording Classes via Zoom

1. Continue a meeting with Zoom.

2. Tap the Log button

3. Study lessons

4. End conference, and submit a link with comprehensive objectives like assignments to the file.

Teaching over Video

Some in-office departments will not be able to deal with video conferencing and the potential difficulties it presents. Here are some tips to help group members conduct Zoom conferences and call seamlessly to make you more comfortable. Set aside some room for your first lesson to expose the students to the Zoom and make sure about their audio and video connections.

Have an objective or schedule by Screen Sharing a paper or slide at the beginning of each lesson. This adds up to students having a clear idea of how the class will proceed, what will be covered, and the tasks they are going to engage in.

- Where to share a Whiteboard, paper, Screen or photograph, seek math problems with whiteboarding, or let participants use annotation.

- Identify items like grammar errors in a paper you share.

- Taking the opportunity to progress the class questions, feedback, and responses.

- Give your users a minute to let them using answers, write in conversation, or be unmuted to ask any questions live.

- Explore web behavior and student standards in the first simulated lesson, then refresh the topics daily.

- Being the presenter, share the initiatives with the class. It helps the students to demonstrate what you are presenting.

- Focus on student's delivery skills as they work. It also encourages learners to hear from each other.

- Use a shared document in the Whiteboard or transcribe it, and let your learners also engage.

- Divide the conversation into smaller units on a given topic. You may use the Breakout Room feature in Zoom on either Pre-assign students to attend classes for a limited period to address issues together.

- Pre-arrange the meeting and silence the microphones of the members upon entry.

- This helps to prevent background noise and allows for your students to focus on the class.

- Aim at the monitor and get the students into eye touch. This tends to establish a more intimate link throughout teaching.

- Take a second to test your students' conversation or video to check-in and receive input from the teachers.

- Talk as though you are connected explicitly to the class while ensuring you are at the proper distance to the microphone for excellent hearing performance.

- Sharing photos, files, or videos while giving a presentation offers students a chance to loosen up or breathe in what you have shared.

- Take a break after you stop debate and encourage the students to participate before moving further.

3.2 Engaging Students during Class

Now that everyone has been thrown into the online teaching environment, teachers have to work out how to involve their learners online as instructors. Many of the first items schools did having daily video sessions with their learners when moving to distance education.

This can differ depending on the learners' ages and the content of the teacher that he/she communicates with the learners, but most instructors soon found that they could not use the same behavior techniques (like closeness) they used in a traditional classroom. This can result in a loss of interest and students' participation with what they are learning to be learned irrespective of gender.

These teaching techniques mentioned below are not supposed to take the place of more comprehensive learning. Although achieved with a combination of distance communication; that kind of teaching methods are usually easier. They e said, to bring the learners into the deeper state of education with a deeper level of awareness. The instructors need to make sure that the kids are involved while having simultaneous interactions and conversations. Any of these techniques require little set-up, whilst others may need more time and resources to make them fully effective. These resources aim to bring students into the lesson/behavior and make them excited and moving forward to the next interactive teaching session.

Though there are lots of video conference approaches out there, the Zoom framework has some of the best immersive functionality and seems to be the most commonly adopted in Higher education universities around the world. Here are some useful strategies you can follow to engage your students during class.

Share Your Screen with Students

Although you can make much of your conversations with the only photo, do not overlook that you do have the opportunity to share with the learners any or all of the display. This can be as easy as answering a topic of the day with a whole PowerPoint presentation. If you have produced a presentation for use in your classroom, do not replicate the strategy, just open it on your sharing screen and use Zoom software like 'lift hand' or the talk room to get a moving backchannel while you go over your slides. A bit of wisdom, verify with your learners what things you have on your laptop, and in your web browser's "personal favorites" tab before you post it. It will help you to estimate your learners' attention towards your class.

Use Whiteboard Feature

You can use the constructed-in whiteboard functionality that works with Zoom if you would not want to display your computer. This function can take some time to become used to, particularly if you are using a cursor or a touchpad. Only go to show your computer and click "whiteboard" to display it. A little more hint – if you have an iPad-like tablet, download the Zoom application and then attend the iPad session. Particularly if you have a good stylus or Apple Pencil, this performs great for drawings. When you are more familiar with Zoom and student aspirations, allow your students to express their perception using the whiteboard function as well. When you are not using Zoom, whether you display your computer with your learners, a website like Classroomscreen.com would have a multitude of features like a whiteboard.

Use Annotation Tools

The annotation tools are another function you might use when posting slides, images, or web pages.

To ensure these functions are allowed by default, you would like to review your user profile. With these techniques allowed, you will be able to text over any image, show some aspects of a website, and allow your students' learning activity much easier.

Create Breakout Rooms for Collaboration

Zoom functions are the opportunity to create breakout rooms for your classes. Unlike the annotation and whiteboard functionality, breakout room construction capability is not allowed by default. You will want to go through your phone settings before utilizing it for your learners to allow that skill. When activated, you can make the Zoom assign learners to rooms either manually or automatically. And if it is allocated randomly, learners can be switched based on group interactions. Before transferring those learners to each room, you may also rename the rooms based on group titles or subjects.

The best thing about such rooms is that they can establish a more relaxed environment than the entire big party's zooming atmosphere. You can move around like the leader and visit rooms to look in on the debate, post an update to all areas or even put a time restriction on them. When you invite children to attend the whole community and finish the breakouts, they will have sixty-seconds to catch up and resume their conversation. It is an effective way to encourage interactive collaboration.

Use Virtual Backgrounds during Class

If you have been in some video conference for the past few months, you have undoubtedly seen all kinds of simulated environments that are insane and enjoyable.

Any practical applications of these simulated environments may, however, occur.

Any examples of using virtual backgrounds may be re-enacting events in life with the right backdrop, choosing a geographical place they could be digitally researching or "visiting," or simply letting students pick either a solid red or green background to demonstrate whether they disagree or agree with a subject easily.

Survey Your Students

You can use the traditional "lift your hand" in the classroom to gain input from students. It is no unique in Zoom as there is a "Lift hand" button open to learners, but some experienced teachers have already pointed out that the chat room will serve as an improvised test as long as it includes short answers. You can still use a platform of Zoom to collect input from a portable device or window tab for better monitoring.

Brainstorm Ideas

One way to connect with learners is to gather input in surveys, but you might also use a virtual collaboration space to allow students to explore and think creatively about public spaces. You could also pair this with the collaboration rooms and provide a subject for team conversation when moving from board and committee. A suggestion here is to build the "walls" or areas so the students can work together, so you have live access to what they are working on. Share the connection to each unit until you have them divided into groups to focus on.

Interactive Presentations

You may share your display with your learners or even your presentations with a platform such as PowerPoint, Briefing, or Microsoft office.

But once you have got them active, use a platform like a Zoom meeting to lead them with you during education. Preferably, this will work well on multiple devices.

You might direct them on one monitor through the introduction. Share the enter code with your participants and then get them to turn to the application when keeping the Zoom application open in the background so that they can listen to your speech as they go along.

Need to Pause

In the classroom, noise can be uncomfortable. Once you glance at more than half a dozen kids on display it is much more uncomfortable. Letting the learners pause and focus during the lesson is crucial. Using a time delay on either a picture, video, or a platform such as ClassroomScreen.com lets participants learn when to interrupt their delay or reflex. Students require relief from extensive teaching during their day, whether they are on a computer or not. If you are holding a fifty-minute lecture online, construct for learners to rest or get a drink of water and keep their mind engaged in a five-minute break.

Brain Breaks

Whether it is for a thoughtful break or just a chance to relax, it is necessary to take breaks during a long lecture. One bit of advice here is that while watching a video via your device speaker systems, ensure you do not really have a headphone on or switch the Zoom sound input by pressing the up-carrot icon next to "Mute" to alter the audio quality range.

Reveal your Answer

It is also good to have a pause from the traditional lecture with everything being virtual when you already have a conference call using screens with the learners. There is a wide range of analog techniques you might use using pencil and paper for your learners. One could post a math question on your computer whilst the students are figuring out the result. Then calculate, and make them immediately show their reactions to their devices.

Record your Class

The standard configuration for users requires a conference session only to be registered by the Zoom conference host to record Zoom, while other meeting members may be allowed to register the meeting.

It usually suggests that host meetings should not enable other members to record a conference with the Zoom.

When a conference host enables a Zoom camera, Zoom declares that "this conversation will be recorded." Once the host finishes the camera, Zoom will declare that "the recording has ended." Any meeting member who enters the meeting conducted will hear a notification from Zoom that the conference will be recorded.

The main reasons for recording a conference on a Zoom involve:

- You plan to upload a digital version of the Zoom for meeting people online for a general or selected community to watch after the event, or you plan to have to reuse the conference (for example, by conducting a public practice session accessible to one audience in a broadcast form for other viewers).

- In the normal format, you might have recorded the conversation anyway, whether you were doing it in person or by phone.

- You suspect that certain important invitees would not be able to attend the meeting, and it would not be enough merely to supply them with a video presentation, notes, observations, or summary after the event.

3.3 Zoom Assignment Setup

Instructors have the option to set up a "Task or Debate Board" in all courses and encourage students to download or submit a file. Large recording files may take up a lot of room in the course or the student's program's submitting region. There has a specific feature for Zoom videos that will guarantee students can reduce their number of files to a minimum.

The application is recognized as the Media Record/Upload method. It would require students to upload five hundred Megabytes files without restricting either the course or the students. Setting up an Assignment or Discussion forum post with these resources, and having the students know the correct way to apply is particularly crucial for the teacher. Do not search the "Data Uploads" box when setting up the assignment because the students would use up much of the course room. Alternatively, you can allow the "Record/Upload Files" feature to avoid massive uploads of files for your task. If you duplicate Assignments from previous classes, you will still need to change them.

Upload Assignment

When you have chosen the "File on this Device" option to document your presentation, using the steps below to transfer your file to an Assignment, your professor will provide the task that is designed to take a Zoom recording. You should not add a Zoom link to a request that has a click "Link Upload". The Role should be designed as described.

1. Select "Send Application" to start Notification.

2. Select "Media track/Upload".

3. Choose the tab "Upload files" then press the button "Download video file".

4. Using the Zoom "Data File" on your Windows.

5. Select on "Deliver Assignment".

3.4 Individual Presentation Setup

Allow the time to customize the external atmosphere before you present a specific presentation. If necessary, prepare a document of the conversation with a microphone because such microphones will eliminate noise not coming from three to five meters away from the mouthpiece.

Use a space where you can shut the door or not be disrupted while minimizing audio from elsewhere in the room. Tiled rooms are recommended over wooden floors to lessen the noise effect in your audiotape. When you capture the video image, sunlight will be coming from in front of you and never behind you to stop putting shadows on your eyes.

One or two crane lamps are lined up behind the screen monitor, and you will be doing this conveniently facing it. Your backdrop should be fascinating but not intrusive, and it does not include a window if the window has both shutters and curtains to obstruct the light. While capturing, mute the mobile phones, email updates, text messages/chats, and other electronic signals. Many vibratory alerts from cell phones are visible when using the smartphone microphone, so you may need to put your mobile phone on a comforter or smooth surface to minimize this.

Setup Individual Presentation

Connect any of the programs that you would not be utilized during the presentation on your device. You may also need to deactivate the "Device Operating System" new email alerts or notices. In your videoed session, this will prevent them from appearing. Place the imaging lens at eye level if you are using a Webphone.

When you are using a tablet, books, a desktop stand, or other surrounding things should be used to boost it. This will guarantee that the audiences in the video get in contact with your eyes.

Zoom Settings

1. Press from the Zoom application on the "Start a conference" icon and connect to the "Audio" meeting.
2. Activate the online camera if necessary.

3. Tap the "Sharing Monitor" button in the Zoom Session lower middle.

4. Pick "Server" and then "Screen Sharing".

5. The menu bar of Zoom can now push up to the top of the display. A green boundary across the Screen you are sharing would be available. This is the area to be recorded.

6. The word or PowerPoint application may need to be enlarged or shrunk, so it takes up an entire display. When you are using your phone, make sure the camera image does not obscure the video.

7. Record your presentation if needed.

Find Presentation

When you are recording a Zoom conference, it will send it to your local device's hard drive. Once the meeting is over, this conference will be converted to a standard.mp4 file format for the Zoom service provider's video playback. Looking in the Downloads folder or inside the Zoom app, you can locate your Zoom recordings by pressing on the following ways:

1. To play back, go to your meeting, beneath the meeting details, press the "Play Video" icon.

2. Tap the "Open" button to find your .mp4 video file on your Screen.

3. Find the folder referring to the date/time of the conference.

4. The video file is often or appropriately called zoom1.mp4.

5. You can rename the video file to facilitate later finding.

3.5 Group Presentation Setup

Zoom has a group presentation feature to enhance teaching facilities during this scenario.

You can conduct group assignments to check the learning of your students and to increase their presentation skills. A team presentation through Zoom is a perfect opportunity for the professor or the whole class to highlight the work. This is necessary to set up each participant's tasks before you start and set up a rehearsal session to rehearse the steps involved. If you record the performance or show live, a crucial step is to work smoothly with the Zoom controls.

Content Sharing

Zoom lets you display your monitor on a laptop, tablet, and handheld computers operating Zoom. By clicking on the "Sharing Screen" icon, the host and the attendant will start screen sharing for presentation. The host does not have to "move the pitch" to communicate or "making someone else a presenter". The host is allowed to "lock screen access" so that no attendant will view the display.

1. Pick the "Connect Display" button inside the toolbar of your conference.

2. You may opt to display your "Desktop" or "External application/window" after clicking the "Display Screen" located in your in-meeting menu.

3. Even when posting a video clip such as Facebook or a locally stored video file, you can choose to share "desktop voice".

Presentation Assistance Tools

You will have the option to use different features during your Screen Sharing. To open the drop-down toolbar by moving your cursor to the top of the screen and selecting "Annotate". Resources for creating annotations include Mouse, Drawing, Edit with text, Screen light, Erase, Coloring, Redo/Undo, Clear, and save. This feature of saving helps you to save all device annotations as a screenshot immediately.

The snapshot and the meeting recording are transferred to the regular meeting tab. You can switch on the "Split Screen for Dual Monitor Option" to display the screen sharing on one display and the participants on the other if you are using a dual monitor configuration. Participant Side Annotation helps any participant to start formatting on an accessed screen. Throughout the upper meeting slider, the participant can use "Annotate".

Control Presentation with your Cursor

Sharing Mouse Controls in Group Presentation can be simple and easy for one person to handle all of the information sharing with numerous persons in a team presentation. For example, the host will monitor the recordings start/stop, while the PowerPoint can be opened on their device by group member one. Other presenters can require the team member one cursor control to track the presentation. For mouse control to be shared;

- Participants must be joining a Windows or Mac conference.

- The participant who exposes his computer shall be on a Laptop or PC.

You may ask the host or the user who is sharing his display for remote control. When the consumer finishes talking, you need to find the slide down toolbar menu at the center's conference screen.

From the drop-down menu, select "wireless remote invitation." It would then submit a message to the host/attendee asking whether he wants you to monitor his display or not.

You can "give mouse/touchpad control" to some other group member who is in the conference while connecting the display in a Zoom meeting.

1. First, the host or member must pick "Share Screen" (Host cannot facilitate screen sharing to display in the meeting with another member).

2. Then, push your mouse up to the top of your conference window/panel to click the panel sharing drop-down button.

3. Click "Give access to mouse/touch screen" and then pick the person to whom you want to grant access.

   1. To start control, the members can click on anywhere on their display.

Duties of a Teacher as Host

As a teacher, the host of the conference has four primary duties:

1. The meeting is arranged via the Zoom application, and the meeting URL is submitted to the other team leaders.

2. Begin/delay/finish documentation of the contents of the discussion during the conference.

3. Download the captured video file to show or edit by teacher or class and share it with other members of the group via Office, cloud storage, or some other platform

4. The Meeting Host can even be liable for screen sharing and material modification during a group presentation, as an alternative.

Participants of the conference must enter the URL Zoom group sent out by the Server.

Participants may opt to have a voiceover statement as the meeting moderator manages the PowerPoint presentations, or each participant may have to share their laptop and monitor information distribution for their portion of the conversation.

What can a Host Control?

Meeting Host also had power over all of the conference's activities and functionality. To use these settings, click "Organize Participants" in the menu bar of your in-meeting zoom (you will need to pull your mouse over the participant's name to see all of the possibilities). The group of Members contains many critical terms to the conference. Tap on the "Further" tab at the "Participants" section at the lower right.

- The host can also recover another Host.

- You could kick out the conference participants.

- You can request other members to record the meeting.

- Immediately silence the members when they join the conference.

- It plays a tone as the members exit the conference and leave.

- You may secure the meeting, and no other members are permitted to participate.

- There are also other choices open when jumping over a single person.

- Pause or question to launch a web camera for the participant.

- Mute/Unmute All meeting participants: you will have the choice (checkbox) to enable the members to unmute or not.

- Other users would not be allowed to access a display when choosing lock screen sharing.

- Make Host: you can grant another participating member permission to be the host of the meeting-after, making another member the host of the conference,

- Change the name set for the audience member.

- Place the student on hold, delete them from the video and audio conferencing.

3.6 Different Teaching Scenarios

For several professors, staff, students, and parents, online digital learning has become modern. While the transformation might not be quick, instructors want to include tools to ensure that students who are using Zoom to build stable and successful virtual classrooms. There are different teaching scenarios that can be helpful in a teacher's decision making in arranging online classes.

Zoom Meetings vs. Zoom Webinars to Host a Class

Both conferences and webinars are excellent opportunities to interact and communicate with huge audiences and also gain useful feedback through registration criteria. But there are important variations between conferences and webinars:

Conferences are structured to be fully immersive, allowing the members to use video and audio, display their computer, and transcribe in a live, engaging environment. Webinars allow you more control in handling the crowd. Webinar participants communicate with the moderator and each other through the question and answers and talk directly, rather than communicating via audio and video. Conferences can be beneficial for a hands-on, interactive learning atmosphere in which students can actively interact with the digital platforms and with each other. Webinars are useful for video lectures where learners can use the Question answer function to listen, display material, and answer questions.

Best Practices for Setting up Virtual Classrooms

Here are a few tips to help you build a healthy and effective interactive classroom:

- Require Passwords: enter a password for a conference or webinar and start sharing it with the students to achieve that only attendees with the password can participate in your digital class.

- Enrollment Require: Enrolment will be required for all conferences and webinars to see if anyone has registered up to attend your class. The registered owner may also be accepted automatically to help decide who will attend the class.

- Activate Waiting Rooms: Waiting Rooms prohibit people from immediately attending a conference, and are allowed by confirmation. Each participant can be accepted separately or all students at once. You will also encourage students who are signing in via your education domains to bypass the Waiting Room, while people who are not part of the domains of your education must be accepted.

- Deactivate screen sharing: Screen sharing configurations are settled for educational users, so only the operator can share a monitor. This prohibits the participants from revealing inappropriate or intrusive information. You may change this configuration or enable in-meeting sharing inside the Security icon to enable your attendants to share information.

- Disable personal chat: The host has the option to lock the conversation so that the members are unable to connect with each other in person. The teacher should also encourage students to speak with them.

- Handle participants: If an unwelcome member has entered the class, delete the member with Security icon settings.

Obtain other tips for handling members on the help forum, including the option to silence participants, interrupt their video, and prevent renaming.

- Lock the group: You can also lock the group directly from the Safety button to discourage any participating members until the meeting starts. Not only does this function keep out unwelcome visitors, but it is also useful for implementing a forgetful system.

Secure Classroom

There is a range of tools and configurations that are allowed by definition and can be used on the go to maintain the protection of your Zoom classrooms. The Protection icon is your all-in-one location for easily discovering and activating safety features within your conference. This role allows for a host or co-host to:

- Join the conference.
- Allow the room to wait.
- Remove members.
- It limits the ability of respondents to display, speak, replace, and transcribe.

Waiting Rooms and conference keys are allowed as an extra layer of protection by definition for unlimited, simple, and individual authorized pro profiles and account holders. The authentication standard for accounts cannot be modified.

Taking Classroom Attendance

One way to take part during the online school is to request confirmation so that you can check the intake sheet and see who enrolled and who really attended. Another way of taking attendance is to initiate a questionnaire during training. You will export the survey report later and see who participated in your class based on who answered the survey.

See All Students on Video

With Zoom in "Galleries Mode," you have the opportunity to see up to forty-nine people on Screen. Only allow this function in video configurations. Click on the left side arrows in "Galleries Display" to open up to one-thousand thumbnails to reveal another forty-nine participants.

Set Up Breakout Rooms for Students

Breakout rooms encourage you to divide your classroom into as many as fifty different classes, perfect for group-based tasks or projects. Attendees have complete audio, video, and networking capability for any breakout room. Also, each room will inform the host when assistance is needed, and the leader will access each of the breakouts to support and respond to questions. For using this function, make sure the conference configurations allow breakout rooms. Then you can also pre-assign learners or auto-assign them into classes.

Who can Annotate, and How?

You have the option to sketch, write, and apply decorations to your digital platforms while you are displaying your Screen. Even the moderator has the option to annotate members on their display. This is a perfect way to keep the students involved and cooperate. You can even use a Whiteboard while displaying your display. This is much like a whiteboard you had to see in your classroom, displaying a blank web screen that you and your assistants will use to collaborate together on issues.

Using Zoom on Chromebook

Hosting and attending conferences on a Chromebook would allow you to access much of the functionality on other computers you would have. What you need to do is to enter your conferences via the Zoom application available in the Chrome web store.

The key drawbacks in a Chromebook are that there is no sampling, whiteboard, description, and motion sensor.

Chapter 4: Benefits of Zoom App and its Comparison with Other Tools

Zoom supports companies of all markets and scales, and it can efficiently scale their network to suit any case of an increase and expenditure. But one of the best aspects of work is to see precisely how much Zoom will affect smaller companies. There are problems specific to starting a private company. Conducting several procedures with only a few employees and a minimal resource, and prioritizing the time and money to make it work effectively can be addressed with the Zoom framework. Communication channels can help a growing company attain its targets and better support its ever-changing needs. Zoom's flexibility and user-friendliness, not to include its segmented pricing and utilization arrangements, simplifies how local business teams handle their resources, improves competitiveness, and grow the enterprise.

4.1 Benefits of Using Zoom

Zoom is a fantastic and famous web-conference choice, with more than one million attendees per day.

You may use Zoom to

- Keep voice call live.

- Analytics of meetings participation, such as biggest sites by minutes of conversation.

- Screen-share conveniently throughout a call.

- Store your meetings and log them using the recording feature.

- You can keep strategy meetings using the smart board functionality on-screen.

- Enable in-depth resources, such as live aid, webchat, telephone support, discussion forums, video guides, and posts.

- Connect on functionalities like Pause and windows media player.

- Start using unlimited plan in which you can host up to a hundred participants in a video call with Zoom's free package.

- Then you can utilize Zoom to operate conferences. You will welcome guests to your session in Zoom that uses a customized registration link.

- You can also save your conference and replay it again, thanks to the Zoom recording functionality.

Here are five things why small companies choose Zoom to support them and by doing so expand their consumer base, sales, and organization overall.

Zoom is Simple to Set Up, Including Usage and to Navigation

You are doing huge stuff, and you mustn't be perhaps one of those operating as aid! Zoom promises easy buying and launch, with no hidden costs. Starting or entering every meeting is one click away, and Zoom allows simple coordination and monitoring of the participants. In short, there is no need for an Information Technology Unit to go out and handle the Zoom.

Industrial Networking with the Squad at Large

Bring the whole team together on camera (up to a hundred regular attendees), or just for a simple one-on-one chat. In low-bandwidth settings, it provides High definition audio and video, so the users can quickly communicate, interact, and function with flexibility.

Single Gathering Site, Zoom Phone, Webinars, and Talk

Using the time wisely for workshops, webinars, phone calls, and talk with a standard answer. Your workers need to use one approach, and they will appreciate you for all of that. The best part: Zoom keeps innovating its product to satisfy growing market needs, so you will never have to think about having another messaging network.

Log in Via Computer Customers, Websites, Meeting Rooms, and Smart Applications

Zoom is all about ease and versatility. Zoom runs smoothly through all of the web browsers, so workers aren't forced into particular computers. You can even inexpensively enable or disable video in any meeting rooms or office space through Zoom Rooms, which are both agnostic software and easy to set up. Or use one of Zoom's all-in-one gadgets that further facilitates how the room interface is installed, handled, and scale- up.

Substantial Value for Money and Financial Return

It is not that long time ago that Zoom was a small company, and everyone knows how essential it is by face-to-face contact to get things accomplished faster and create connections. Zoom lets you do exactly that with a lot of functionality for video chat bundled into one small monthly payment. Their implementations with Google and Microsoft will simplify your conferences. Their App Store has more than two-hundred integrations with pioneering applications such as Slack and PayPal to increase Zoom's strength.

Zoom Cons

But zooming is still not a great tool. If you are thinking about utilizing Zoom, you must understand a few details about depending on the network. Next, because you are paying by the Zoom server, it can get costly for bigger teams.

The expense depends on the choice of rate, such as the company vs. sector vs. a corporation. Pro starts at fifteen dollars per host per month and moves up to nineteen dollars per host per month. Second, though Zoom has creative tools, including white-boarding, voting, and motion sensors and users say that it is hard to use. Another downside for Zoom is the low, inconsistent quality of the footage, according to several clients. Zoom imagery is frequently distorted and blurred. The performance of the video and audio will continue to deteriorate of being unusable.

Benefits of Zoom Phone

Perhaps the Zoom device's most significant advantage is just how simple it is to use. The method is programmed to be as usable as most of the Zoom interface, so no advanced program has to be downloaded to use it. You can quickly switch from videos to voice service with Zoom Phone-find the communication technique that matches you. Benefits involve:

- **Simplicity for Everyone:** whenever you tap on your Zoom file, your smartphone feature will appear next to your Conference and Message options. The only tap on your phone, type the name or telephone number of an individual, and you are ready to go. It is straightforward and easy.

- **Link to other services:** You can also link the SIP approach to other networks. Via a few of the world's most popular cloud calling systems, it is easier to handle your call routing choices.

- **Bring Your Own Carrier (BYOC):** Zoom is dedicated to inventing with its users as quickly as practicable to offer features that fit the whole Zoom community. The Bringing Your Own Carrier guarantees that you can control Zoom Phone's benefits from your established IP based phone jackets.

- **Complete autonomy:** Zoom allows Zoom Phone as versatile and feasible for target consumers, due to its functionalities and "Bring Your Own Carrier" (BYOC) accessibility. According to Zoom's Head of business development, the solution also ensures that Zoom Phone will be used in any region-even though public councils are not yet accessible.

4.2 Zoom vs. Skype Meet

Skype, as well as Zoom, are two of the most suggested communication channels for virtual workers. You could even hold voice calls, conversations, and broadcast conferences or webinars on both operating systems. And if you are looking for a new means of helping you do all these things, then you will probably consider both technologies. Overall, the distinctions among Zoom and Skype might not seem massive. But the ability to accept one over the other could still affect your team significantly. From one distant group, quality developers know that every platform fits into different requirements. And so, knowing the pros and cons is crucial to your choice.

 It is indeed contextual when it relates to which system is best for teamwork and communication. Zoom and Skype each have benefits and drawbacks, which can help or damage your group's capabilities to engage efficiently. Overall, Skype is an outstanding tool for communication. Not only is Skype famous with business owners, but it is also a powerful tool to communicate with friends, family, colleagues, and customers around the globe. It could be a game-changer for businesses that use Microsoft products and Skype, especially when considering all of the great content of Skype.

With Skype, you can:

- Use the Internet, hold conference calls, and support private, household, and foreign demands.

- Perform annotations, screen sharing and file transfer, which supports big files.

- White-board, posting a poll, and holding a question-answer session.

- Start with the paid app that works perfectly for lesser teams.

- Invest in windows 10, which will soon include Skype, and get additional business characteristics such as Microsoft Word and spreadsheets office apps.

- The best advantage is the link to Microsoft Staff, allowing it a network you can seamlessly combine with software that your company might already be utilizing.

- Skype is outstanding as a stand-alone networking platform but much better when using it in the business system with Microsoft Package. You can utilize this in some fantastic companies and find a helpful tool for collaboration.

Video Quality

Video consistency is among the most important things to remember. During the meeting, you would not want to appear pix-elated, so you will be pleased to hear that both Zoom and Skype are trying to take advantage of rising to 1080p capture. Your software and access to data needs to be up to the challenge. Skype suggests a 1.2Mbps link for high-definition communications, although, at its peak levels, Zoom is a little more difficult at 3Mbps.

The only significant difference is that by design, the Zoom does not allow 1080p sizes. Instead, the configurations need to be updated manually, and the team has to switch on High definition or higher resolutions at the edge.

Otherwise, you are going to use 720p footage (which is also fantastic, undoubtedly). As for the quality of the recording, this can rely more on your mic. You should find out the best USB headsets.

Participants Limit

In the Zoom vs. Skype debate, how big your party is, can significantly affect your choice. Skype's Online Market edition restricts you to fifty users. In the meantime, paying Microsoft Team packages allows up to three hundred people to participate in a unified video call. However, these figures are small relative to the Zoom's. The free package of Zoom Conferences lets you launch video calls with up to a hundred attendees.   If you have a big business and need more than three hundred people to make video calls, Zoom is your best option. Skype also released a new product called "Meet Now" which does not allow people to sign up for both the product or install the video conference app.

The new functionality appears to be borrowing from Zoom and often enables users to attend meetings via their websites despite needing to submit in or update their software. Both Zoom vs. Skype create a particular reference for joining a video conference that everyone can exchange. If you are the organizer of the meeting, you can invite everyone, irrespective of whether they are Zoom or Skype consumers. When in the call, customers can take advantage of the full variety of components that both platforms have to provide. This could support if your friends do not necessarily want to register for one.

Other Features

The technology of Zoom and Skype has a somewhat similar collection of applications. These include screen sharing, video sessions, online storage, whiteboard, shared calendars, a phone meeting, etc.

Yet zooming is overall a great option for built-in functionality. People look at Skype for having features such as effectively addressing URLs, discussion sessions for group separation of members, the simulated raising of hands, and more.

Security

Zoom and Skype both have industry-leading protections and end-to-end authentication. Still, recently Zoom has been at the forefront of privacy issues, prompting them to suspend new functionality for ninety days. Through protection improvements, strengthening security, adding the option to uninstall personal conference IDs, and battling Zoom bombing, the company can't get a break when more than five million hacked identities are sold online. For Zoom, it is not a great time, and the privacy-conscious of you would like to remain with Skype for some time. Meanwhile, the organization continues to struggle with updates against the Zoom bombing. There is still end-to-end authentication in the development, but upgrades are underway.

Pricing

Zoom's free plan is fantastic, but you may be dragged down by the limits of one-hundred users and forty minutes. People that need more should ask for a monthly membership, which is charged. Microsoft Teams arrive with the enterprise edition of Skype. Considering that Microsoft Teams comes with many other services, such as Microsoft Office teamwork and exposure to advanced features, this means people can see more benefit in this. Prices do start at five dollars, but this is per customer. You will need to think about your needs and do the calculations and see what is most cost-effective.

Skype Cons

Skype has technological setbacks that do not allow it to achieve its highest potential. Skype is reported to seize up despite having good audio and video than the Zoom.

Skype is freezing and creating disruptions in the video. People often have to terminate calls and request again. It is not decent enough and is throwing away the atmosphere of the conference. Users also remember that Skype is hard even to get support or advice, which is shocking because it is all within Microsoft's framework. Additional drawbacks include how much space the app uses up, accessibility problems, and buggy Skype, difficult to use Interface. It is one of the best platforms out there, but Skype leaves many people waiting for its drawbacks.

Final Thoughts

If you pick a communication tool and distinguish between Skype and Zoom, you will note that all of these apps have their strengths. For companies looking for a cohesive business strategy, Skype is great. For teams with regular video calls and workshops, using zoom is a perfect choice.

4.3 Zoom vs. Google Meet

Zoom Meet and Google Meet are business-oriented applications. All have their share of customers, which increases throughout this situation of even more citizens working at home. If you are considering registering for one of these but do not understand which one to go with, designers have protected you. In the Zoom vs. Google Hangouts, designers compare the two i.e. Zoom and Hangouts to find out which one comes out on top.

Similarities

Zoom as well as Google Hangouts Both have much of the same simple idea. Both are platforms for conferencing and enable one-on-one conferences and community meetings. They provide various services, such as the option to access a conference via a link or by smartphone.

Conferences can be accessed on both desktops and laptops and iOS computers, with Android and Apple applications providing both facilities.

Users would be able to silence their microphones during a chat and switch off their screens if they want further security. Often, the host and the individual who controls a meeting can silence the participants' microphones. Anyone who's been at a large community gathering online understands how important it is. There is still the one individual who listens to a conference call or has kids in the background crying. Both systems now allow screen sharing that is a must-have conference and meeting feature and instant messaging. The consumer will send messages for others to see on a community platform. It is useful for answering queries and exchanging files throughout a conference.

The last noteworthy shared feature is the ability to record conferences. When you have a great staff, this is a must, as it helps workers who have skipped a briefing to search it out later and get up to full speed. But not all schedule Hangouts Meet offers involve this function, which will be addressed in more depth in the next portion.

Differences

Zoom as well as Google Hangouts Meet are quite different apps serving different audiences considering their similarity. Zoom is far more sophisticated, providing tons of features which depend on your requirements might not be a huge deal for you.

Zoom lets audiences digitally lift their hands by clicking a button to avoid several individuals from communicating at the same moment. The host then decides who needs to talk first and offers them the stage.

The app allows polling, as well. These can be generated and exchanged in forums, enabling attendees to change their ballots on the issue.

Among other features, Zoom is useful for voting on multiple business-related judgments. Other worth noting functionalities in Zoom include Virtual Backdrop, which helps you to set a picture or video as your backdrop during a conference. This is a perfect choice for people who would not want to see the interior of their home. Then there is fix up the "Appearance", which is simply a mask that helps smooth the face, making this important meeting even more flawless.

There is another feature of direct messaging which enables people to send a personal message during a conference to a friend. Hangouts Meet offers hardly any of the features listed so far. The video conferencing software on Google is all about convenience. It focuses mainly on the specific functionality that firms require to host meetings digitally. The only Hangouts Meet function not accessible on Zoom is live subtitles, which show the phone discussion text. Just bear in mind that it helps English only and that the subtitles will not appear on videos.

While talking about the recording theme, it is essential to note that this functionality is included on all Zoom packages, including unlimited ones. Hangouts Meet users have access to it, though, only if they register for the costliest service. As per the number of users it serves, Zoom still has a huge edge on Hangouts Meet. The program's far more costly package and covers conferences of up to five hundred people, and more can be included for an extra cost. Google Hangouts Meet's maximum bound is for two hundred and fifty users.

Pricing

Unlike Hangouts Meet, Zoom has a free way of selling. It enables up to a hundred attendees per conference, allows unrestricted one-on-one conferences, and provides several functionalities. These include the option to capture a discussion, turn off microphones from the attendees, display your phone, lift your hands when you wish to talk and, among many others, use interactive viewpoints. It does have a major drawback, though, which is that community sessions will only run up to forty minutes. Moving up to one of the business's paying policies is the way of getting rid of this restriction. Pricing is competitive, from just fifteen dollars per host.

Although Zoom is a separate application, it is not like Google Hangouts Meet. It is compatible with Google G Suite's business-oriented package, which contains many other utilities, including the option to use Gmail as a corporate email account (also without advertisements), links to features such as Hangouts Chat, also extra cloud storage for Google Drive. Pricing begins at six dollars a month and requires up to a hundred individuals to attend a group. The amount goes up to one hundred and fifty in line for the next package, costing you at least twelve dollars a month. However, the most affordable alternative is twenty-five dollars a month, which requires up to two-hundred and fifty people per conference. Remember that all video conferencing platforms are distributed per server, not per user. This ensures that any person who attends a conference or webinar does not have to pay a monthly fee. People may enter for free, but a monthly fee needs to be charged by the conference owner or the one that establishes up a conference.

Final Thoughts

There is no question that, in general, Zoom is the best choice. In addition to providing many more services, it also has an unlimited option available, which is ideal for one-on-one conferences as well as brief community meetings (under 40 min.), which does not indicate that it is a safer choice for you.

If your appointments do not get in the path of the basic version constraint, go for Zoom. Paying for what you can get for free does not make any sense. If the forty-minute restriction of Zoom is an issue for your company, then you will have to pay the money. In a video conference platform, choosing which of the two providers you can spend your money on and that can get down to what you are searching for.

Zoom would hardly split the bank because it begins at just fifteen dollars a month. But if you do not care about additional pricing of Zoom and what you want is a simple to use the conferencing app, Hangouts Meet might be the best choice for you. It is cheaper too, only coming in at six dollars a month. You will need to remember all the additional privileges that you receive from a G-Suite profile. One of the several facilities used in Google Hangout plan is Hangouts Touch, while Zoom is a separate application.

4.4 Zoom vs. Microsoft Teams

Zoom is a pioneer (and potentially the highest-profile since its Initial public offering in April) in the communication business, addressing digital networking at all endpoints through their cloud network for multimedia, audio conferencing, sharing, messaging, and webinars. Microsoft Teams is the all-encompassing development application integration with Microsoft and a single messaging platform that integrates workshops, messages, calls, and cloud storage with the 365-technology system.

Microsoft Teams and Zoom all converge and perform at a very high degree with the way they provide a wide range of remote facilities and UC communications technologies.

Features

Both Zoom and Teams support online meetings, conversations, calls, screen sharing, and document management where technologies are concerned. Microsoft's collaboration of Departments and its Office 365 platform is the distinction between the two. This makes it easier for Microsoft Teams to be a one-stop-shop for certain organizations. It also facilitates smooth communication and transfers files during conference. But going some way to complement the introduction with Microsoft's Office365, Zoom offers a wide-ranging relationship and a collection with technological functionalities. Zoom, as a corporation, is a far younger entity than Microsoft's powerhouse. Still, it continues to succeed in its ambitious strategy, and since it doesn't have to think about handling (and ultimately migrating) several existing customers at the grounds.

UX (User Interface)

In Microsoft Teams vs. Zoom controversy, the Interface and interaction are really where Zoom succeeds. Zoom users are all raving about the simple implementation and the potential to function effectively up and running with little or no instruction or IT helps. Microsoft Teams faces a bigger problem as customers need to get to grips with how to communicate in various networks and departments, integrate file sharing, as well as the other Office 365 apps built into departments, particularly if the complete range of shared work-stream features built into Teams explicitly allows it to give a larger field of use and possibilities (and therefore a greater value) than zoom.

Room System

When the comparisons between Zoom and Teams continue to become highly decentralized, one field of distinct separation is the "space structures" built within an enterprise.

A space layout can vary from a basic backfield room into a deluxe meeting room for executives. They decompose all you need to learn regarding room systems like comparing Microsoft Teams vs. Zoom room systems in their webinar on UC Meeting Rooms. Although both provide system control, touch upgrades, mobile companion apps, and dual-screen space support, Zoom has the additional advantage of tracking participants and Teams with distance recognition. Another discrepancy between Zoom and Microsoft Teams would be that Zoom certifies all integrated systems and software suppliers, while Teams approve only the technology systems.

Pricing

Microsoft Teams and Zoom both provide a free version of the program, adding more premium options for paying plans. Microsoft Teams' unlimited version includes restricted chat and teamwork, applications, and games for communication, conferences, calls, and safety. Two big features that are missing with the unpaid app include employee tools or support from Microsoft. Zoom's free plan contains conferences that can accommodate up to a hundred participants (with a group discussion limit of forty minutes), unlimited 1:1 conference, customer meetings, clip and web services attributes, group support tools, and protection. Microsoft's Paid plan is marginally cheaper per consumer than the equivalent paid plans for Zoom, but they are charged equally with their business services.

UC Telephony

The capacity to create calls at an organizational level is critical, especially for video, audio, conferencing, and communicating business analytics. This range of features was originally a fortress of Microsoft, as Zoom did not originally have an option for the telephone system.

Microsoft handles UC Telephony with Microsoft phone network and Calling Schedules or Direct Filtering with Microsoft telephone network. Because of Teams' potential to "port" this whole sub-category straight from its Skype for Business roots, enterprise speech has been a major priority for Teams since Microsoft expects to use Teams to substitute Skype for Business. Direct routing facilitates among SIP trunk and an SBC using Microsoft Phone Framework. Teams can be equipped with approved nodes for caller ID, Microsoft contact information, dial schedules, call lists, and auto assistants.

The Zoom Phone is the key to a business voice. This very recent yet increasingly growing older cloud phone infrastructure features smart call routing and maintenance, auto-attendant/Interactive voice, integration with common endpoints, voicemail and chat logs, caller ID, and mobile dialing, plus call logging. It features apps on both desktop and handheld computers, as do Microsoft Teams. Besides, Zoom's "Bring Your Own Carrier" project is a direct reaction to Teams' Direct Routing capabilities, empowering Zoom Phone organizations to exploit existing PSTN network companies in many world markets.

Integrations

Integrations are a big part of Information technology security services, and Zoom has rendered them a key feature of their UCaaS space service. Integrations improve and expand the platform's functionality and help users becoming much more efficient when using the software.

Many younger consumers still have an app store experience, ensuring that they are easy to discover applications that can make their everyday life smoother and more productive. This is another huge element in the controversy over Microsoft Teams vs. Zoom.

The best win for Microsoft Teams is its tight, built-in incorporation with Office 365 applications. Still, apart from that, Microsoft Teams have more than seventy integrations that include fare processing solutions, polls, environment, media, etc. Integrations, usually, in the case of Microsoft, tend to put client data onto its own network. On another side, Zoom is also applied to other channels as an extension. The way Zoom and Slack function together would be a perfect example of that. In contrast to the Slack application, Zoom has more than a hundred integrations, such as an Office 365 inclusion.

Final Thoughts

There is no clear solution or leader, but the final decision depends on your own company's desires and conditions. Indeed, in many situations, Microsoft Teams and Zoom collaborate to work together effectively, rather than pushing an either-or scenario. In reality, we are progressively seeing big companies on both Teams and Zoom choosing to "standardize." Microsoft Teams is great for internal teamwork, while Zoom is mostly favored for outside work as with clients or guest suppliers. Since they communicate with each other, it is simple for users to build specific situations where to use when. In the new global world, Multiplatform is becoming, even more, the prevailing trend. Designers have found in a recent study that eighty percent of consumers use different channels for social applications. Even if both Zoom and Microsoft Teams are not officially distributed within the business, there may be different uses in various divisions of both applications.

Chapter 5: Tips and Tricks to Use Zoom for Effective Teaching

Tips and tricks for using Zoom effectively have been described in detail in this chapter. To use Zoom;

- Find a well-lit, peaceful venue.

- Make sure no ambient noise is present i.e. fans, vacuum cleaners, heavy music, etc.

- Ensure sufficient illumination is provided by using the video from the webcam.

- Use Headset or Wireless earbuds.

- Before the meeting starts, test the audio and video camera.

- Inform Zoom classrooms or conferences students and let them realize that they can connect the link via Zoom, share the Zoom URL via address, calendar activity, updates, or some other shared virtual world that anyone can use.

- Plan Google Calendar conferences.

- Set standards and make the students aware of the class goals. For example, "we'll discuss your queries after I teach for fifteen minutes," "the Supervisor will track the text conversation and answer questions at 11:00" etc.

- Register session of the Zoom category to the server.

- The recording will be instantly translated with machine-based subtitles. You will modify the recording to remove mistakes after the conference.

- It is necessary for learners with hearing difficulties to get a lecture capture or photo titled as quickly as possible after recording.

5.1 Pre-Schedule your Class

If you have been through a meeting with your coworkers, you should focus on the preparations you've taken into the workshop. You need to be comfortable for your conference to prevent wasting your time; therefore, schedule your conference in advance. If you are going to schedule an online class or training, pre-schedule your class and send links to your participants to prepare their minds for the upcoming class. This will help students to be more focused on your class.

5.2 Have a Teaching Agenda Set

Before holding a session or class, pre-plan your teaching agenda so that it can save you time. Setting a meeting or class agenda can help you to be more professional and focused during class timing. Team participants will have problems actively contributing if they do not know whether they can pay attention, provide input, or be part of the conversation process. If people believe that they are interested in making decisions because you want their input, the conversation's conclusion may anger everyone. Before the meeting, notifications are better reserved and perused, utilizing a specific portion of the document to answer participants' questions. If the intention is to make a judgment, state the rule which governs the decision. Setting up a conference schedule will help you organize the conference ahead so there will be more time to understand, rather than worrying about what to do next.

5.3 Sharing Screen with Students

Although you do not have connections to a projection, Zoom App on your computer always helps you make projections and bring group members.

You can launch a screen-share by pressing the Alt + S keys on the keyboard, which will break off the view from your camera to reveal anything you want to project on your phone to all meeting attendees. This is helpful if you attempt to show a large graphic in a conference or wish to view a PowerPoint Table. If you are the host, you can offer an even more elegant appearance by having additional adjustments.

When you are working on a group, you can even collaborate using an interactive whiteboard. If you are in a conference, press on the Sharing Screen icon and then pick Whiteboard. After that, description tools will emerge, which will enable you to sketch programs and concepts with colleagues. You can store Whiteboard meetings as individual files or merge them into a single File. Click the arrow inside the "Save" key in the menu on the "Whiteboard" panel, and you can pick the size you want.

Be sure you've got what you will discuss in line and are good to go before the conference begins. That way, when you touch the Sharing Screen icon, you can move into the PowerPoint presentation display, Excel database, or web page automatically. This way, you do not expose any sensitive information that you may have stored on your laptop, and you will look good in the system.

5.4 Mute Student's Microphone to Avoid Interruption

This is a simple law of conference calls, but it needs repeating, no matter what program you use. A mute voice, while you are not speaking, helps to eliminate background noise for distraction. You should set yourself up with your settings to be instantly silenced when you attend a meeting. This feature is very helpful in delivering your lectures to your class if you are a teacher.

You can ask your students to turn off their microphones when they are not speaking to avoid background noise. If they want to ask any questions, they can use Zoom's "Raise your Hand" feature.

5.5 Ensure Meeting Settings to Save Class Time

Owing to technological complications, it is highly common for video conferences to be postponed or disrupted. Turn on your computer to ensure it does not happen and verify if Zoom is functioning properly at least ten to fifteen minutes before starting a meeting. And if anything goes wrong, notify your conference manager as soon as possible (unless you are the organizer – tell your attendees of the same). Although undertaking a review before each meeting can feel agonizing, it is way better than being humiliated or irritated whenever anything goes wrong throughout your video conference. Ensuring meeting settings can help you save your class time if you are going to arrange a class or webinar.

5.6 Reporting other Participants

It is now possible to communicate on the calls to the members who are not invited or cause problems. Along with deleting them from the line, you can now complain to the Zoom Confidence and Safety team to deal with device misuse.

In the meantime, this would effectively block them from the network and also interfere with other calls. To do this, press on the "Conference" position button and then press "Report".

5.7 Automatically Schedule Meetings and Let People Know About Them

If you are running many meetings with customers, for example, but do not have a secretary, you may want to link your planning application, zoom, and calendars. For example, suppose someone schedules an activity in a scheduling system. In that case, Zappier will generate a new meeting request immediately and add it to any software you are using for your private calendar. To bring this optimization even more efficiently, you can add a phrase that communicates the conference's details with your team via a messaging application like Slack. Any time a new project meeting starts in Zoom, the Zoom link is immediately posted to Slack's proper channel.

5.8 Create Recurring Meetings

Zoom lets you build repetitive sessions. You can configure the call parameters you like before and have it in there wherever you want to connect, and you can enter the calling each time that uses the same Address. Only sign in to the Mobile Zoom application, press the calendar, press the Repeat button, and pick a re-occurrence. See Zoom's Information page on arranging meetings for more information on regular meetings in particular and all-conference configurations.

5.9 Collect Information from Attendees

You can also obtain information for yourself from conference members when you start the session, in addition to having an attendance list. For instance, you would want to ask participants to include their name, business association, or profession. To gather this information, you will then need enrollment, which is a choice available in the Zoom web application's "My Meetings" page. You should then set up a questionnaire that participants will have to fill out before they can enter. Zoom offers basic fields for the application form, such as title and business association, which you apply using the checkbox.

Only hop over to the tab named Customized Queries to introduce new queries or areas.

Even so, if you are using Zoom to operate a webinar-like multimedia experience, you may want to enroll participants using a form online or an event planning application. Technology is a perfect way to ensure anyone who signs up for the webinar can automatically be enrolled in Zoom. These pre-constructed whacks are suitable to get started with Zoom.

5.10 Record Zoom Calls as a Video

Zoom allows you to capture video phone calls. However, you need the authorization to use it. The host of the conference would have to make filming in configurations. It is worth testing the configuration of your account to ensure that recording is allowed before you begin.

- Sign in to the account at Zoom.

- Tap to open Account Setup/Configuration.

- Move to the Login tab and press Video Recording.

Note that Zoom administrators can enable recording for anyone, users, or classes. There is more information on this storage configurations. To record a meeting with Zoom, you need to choose how to use the regional or cloud alternative. Local means that you save the file format on your device or in another storage site instead. Zoom saves the videos for you in its online storage using the Internet to pay subscribers exclusively. But you will need Zoom with mac OS, Linux, or Windows to film images. When filming a conference and choosing Report to the Server, the video and voice messages are stored in the Zoom folder.

When the calling to zoom starts, you can see an opportunity to capture at the screen's end. Simply clicking on the recording lets you capture in the database or remotely.

If you cannot see the recording feature, search your custom web configuration (under My Conference Configuration) or have your server administrator activate it. You can transfer the video files to a desktop or view them from a server. During the conference, you may also see which members are observing the conference, and once the panel is registered, it will also be informed to others on the board. Whenever the conversation is over, Zoom will turn the recording directly into a functional MP4 video format.

5.11 Removing Background Noise

Zoom has setups that make it possible to create the microphone on your call and delete inappropriate and unpleasant ambient noise. Press through the configuration to enable this, and then select the audio choices. In it, you can see a drop-down button to "delete ambient noise". You may incorporate differing degrees of resistance here.

The maximum will reduce as many as possible, minimizing problems with fan sounds and barking dogs.

Simultaneously, the low concentrations will also encourage you to play ambient music and videos on a cooled-out informal call. There are other technical solutions if the created-in noise reduction would not be enough.

5.12 Improve Your Microphone Quality

If you do not have a completely quiet workplace to operate from, you may consider that things are a little loud with your conversations, which is less than efficient. There is a software program operated by AI that can remove ambient noise from the conversations. If you have installed the software, you can notice your sound output enhanced, and your conferences are even friendlier.

5.13 Use Virtual Backgrounds to Improve View

If you'd like to jazz things up a little but do not want certain users to see your house's hideous mess on the video conference, then there's great news as Zoom provides digital backgrounds. Those would be the illustrations for your calls, including items like room, landscapes, and views on the coast. You can also download a screenshot of something you want to configure the backdrop with Zoom simulated backgrounds. It is available for iPhone as well as desktop computers.

Getting started with digital Zoom backgrounds is pretty straightforward. For example, on a PC or Mac, just launch your Zoom file, click at the center on the "Settings" icon, and pick "Visual Backdrop" from the menu bar. Zoom has certain simulated backgrounds to it.

Tap on the one you want to be using. Press on the text box over and to the right of the example backgrounds if you want your model, select a picture from your camera, and then download it.

You can bring a digital backdrop to a conference, too. Press on the arrows next to the clip icon on the bottom in your Zoom window, pick "use a virtual backdrop," and then the same Virtual backdrop screen will appear.

The organization suggests using a long exposure and a decent camera to achieve the best results, but a simulated backdrop can also be used without a handheld camera. You could also use simulated surroundings to zoom in on the camera. Go to your profile, and attend a meeting from your computer. Then press on the three dots at the end of the screen and press the button "more". Tap on "digital backdrop," then pick the context you would like to use.

5.14 add filters to your Zoom Calls

As well as simulated backgrounds, the use of filtering will liven up the Zoom calls. They come in two sizes and can be seen in the same environment as simulated backgrounds. You may decide to either add different basic colors to your camera or add cartoon characters to your picture from multiple Snapchat-eques modifiers. This may not be suitable for company calls, but they can make it more fun with relatives and friends.

5.15 Co-Host Calls

There might be more than one individual at the head of meetings. A Public relations representative may choose to co-manage a conference with an employee, or a group with more than one leader may choose the co-host instead of preferring one member over another. A teacher may like to conduct a class with a co-teacher. Whatever the situations are, you may launch a call to the Zoom and have only one person in charge.

To use the co-hosting software, you should first allow it in the "Conference Configuration" for Zoom. Check the "Meetings" tab and pick the "Co-host selection". Then check for your co-host to enter when you begin a conference, and attach the individual by tapping on the right side to display when you move your cursor over their picture box. Conversely, you will go to the "Attendees" slot, pick "Control Members", swing over the title of the co-host, and choose as much to find the choice in "Making Co-host".

5.16 Share and Annotate on Mobile

While at the conference, you can exchange files directly from the computer and use the whiteboard feature on your computer by typing your hand remarks.

To annotate when displaying the virtual screen with someone else, select "Display Options" from the bottom of the Zoom range, then click "Annotate". A toolbar will show with all your annotation options-for example, word, insert, button, etc. This will help you in teaching your class.

5.17 Give Attendees a Waiting Room

Zoom lets participants join a video conference with or without the operator. Often small groups prefer this alternative so that they can chit-chat for several moments before the conference formally starts. However, in some cases, getting participants in a simulated space together may be in bad management, preparing for you to proceed. A simpler alternative is to create a digital waiting room where visitors sit on pause unless you let everyone in one by one in the same period. How you allow a waiting room is specifically based on the sort of accounts, you have. However, once you establish a meeting, you will configure what the attendants can see while awaiting your entrance.

5.18 Customize your Preferences

You can configure your expectations in your Zoom application and will extend to any video conference you attend. Both of the favorites are changing camera preferences: click "Change my look" to apply a mask to your monitor so that you do not have to put on a foundation (or bath) when you attend a Zoom Meeting from away, and click "Switch off my camera when you enter a conference" so that your face does not appear accidentally on a massive projection screen if you attend an all-hands meeting.

5.19 Sync Zoom with Slack

If your company wants Slack for real-time collaboration, the device manager should combine Zoom and Slack for quick on-the-fly conference calls. If you or a group member is working overseas and want to explore a complex topic by text alone, this may be a problem. Instead of scheduling a Zoom meeting on your planner, you can enter "/zoom" into Slack, and a conference connection will appear immediately for you and your colleague to engage in your Slack chat.

5.20 Pair Zoom with the Right Video Conferencing Camera

Zoom is such a common technology tool for conference calls because it is so simple to use: when it is installed, you need a couple of taps to begin talking to the teammates. To have a better experience for respondents in the co-located and centralized video conference, select video audio and video camera for the Zoom Room, guaranteeing that members in the Meeting feel involved and representative of a discussion.

The comparative guide to video conferencing will help you determine which camera could be the right choice for your squad.

5.21 React with Emoji on Screen

If you are silenced at a conference, you can always let the owners understand your thoughts with emoji responses. To connect without disturbing the conference, give a friendly smile or a cheering emoji (these responses have a naturally pale skin by design, but you can change it on the mobile browser).

Press the Emotions tab at the base of the conference screen (in the same section as silence video and audio, to the left) to respond to a meeting and pick the result you wanted. After five seconds, Emoji disappears completely. If the meeting's moderator allows for the nonverbal input option, members will put a symbol such as a raised hand beside their name for communication. Any individual would have the chance to get input from each other.

5.22 Host more than Hundred People

If you have a party of over a hundred people to host for business or training, you must move to a private account that is paid. Upgrading to the top tier (Corporation Plus) allows the user to access up to a thousand people.

5.23 Keep Unwanted Guests out of Meetings

With increasing numbers of students and staff switching to Zoom and other remote conferencing sites during this crisis, a disturbing new pattern has appeared in web conferencing: "Zoom bombing." Thinking of it as photobombing where someone discovers or suspects your conference Address, hops into your conversation unannounced, and gets on display.

Zoom has thoughtfully shared some advice in a twitter message, so here's the simplistic explanation of what you should do as a host to avoid abuse of such a type:

- Do not post your session ID online, and do not use your private session ID if you conduct a community hearing; instead, use a completely random meeting ID.

- Using the waiting room option to make sure you can get into the conversation with the people you meet.

- Limit conferences to those logging in with Zoom. If you want to be much tougher, you may also limit your conference to those whose personal emails use a specific domain (such as your business or educational institutions).

- Protect screen distribution to staff without permission.

- Lock sessions are now starting to discourage new members from entering upstream.

If you follow these guidelines and someone still speaks during a call, note that hosts at any moment will (and therefore should) silence disruptive speakers and have the authority to boot everyone out of the conference.

5.24 Conferences at your comfort

You have the opportunity to open an immediate conference or a regular meeting. When you plan a conference, you will be given a Personal conference ID to share or distribute. You, as a presenter, have extra benefits to track or disable conference attendees. Zoom lets you make MP4 recordings over the entire catch and give plug-ins for internet explorer and Outlook. Please be assured everything you post, whether via a laptop or a cell phone usage, is of the finest standard.

You can also make optimization and allow audio switch for uploading the images. Besides all this, attendees choose to raise hand electronically for authorization to ask a question or chat with the group. And using break communities for the Zoom conference style, hosts can specify short community cooperation times without stopping or relaunching the conference.

Conclusion

Our lifestyle has changed entirely in the last few months. We have also switched from social events to social space, from long corporate sessions in uptight meeting rooms to interactive conversations of simulated backgrounds. As a result, several goods and services to Zoom conference calls were thrown into the public spotlight front and center. Today, consumers prefer innovations that deliver comfortable, trouble-free experiences. They don't have to give in to a web of clunky work requests. From its early days, Zoom has taken on the concept of making visual conversations as to its mission easy and cost effective, and the constant attention of the firm paid off. The firm has experienced rapid growth, and the name has become associated with video conferencing in the cloud.

Apart from removing the conventional cost-effective difference between in-person and virtual sessions, the real advantage of video conferencing consists in incorporating the human touch to create the confidence that is essential to any profitable company. Zoom has many different and exciting features that other applications do not have. Uniqueness in Zoom software has enabled it to be the most prevalent in the past few months especially for the education system and teachers who have been making the best use of Zoom App. Video-conferencing with Zoom is easy and beneficial. Its features are attracting more of its customers. They are using Zoom for their different types of meetings like office, educational, political, etc. After all the above descriptions, it is clear that Zoom is the best application for you to start scheduling your meetings as a teacher, officer, or staff member.

CPSIA information can be obtained
at www.ICGtesting.com
Printed in the USA
BVHW090950060521
606416BV00008BA/1013